Angela Murray went out to Guatemala during her gap year to work with street children. She then spent three years working with Toybox, before moving to join the London-based Consortium for Street Children (CSC). Angela has now rejoined Toybox and is a sought-after speaker on the subject of street children and justice. She attends Soul Survivor Church in Watford.

Through the Eyes of a
Street Child

Amazing Stories of Hope

Angela Murray

MONARCH
BOOKS

Oxford, UK & Grand Rapids, Michigan, USA

First published in the UK in 2006 by Monarch Books
(a publishing imprint of Lion Hudson plc),
Mayfield House, 256 Banbury Road, Oxford OX2 7DH.
Tel: +44 (0)1865 302750 Fax: +44 (0)1865 302757
Email: monarch@lionhudson.com
www.lionhudson.com

ISBN-13: 978-1-85424-779-7 (UK)
ISBN-10: 1-85424-779-4 (UK)
ISBN-13: 978-0-8254-6136-1 (USA)
ISBN-10: 0-8254-6136-7 (USA)

Distributed by:
UK: Marston Book Services Ltd, PO Box 269,
Abingdon, Oxon OX14 4YN;
USA: Kregel Publications, PO Box 2607,
Grand Rapids, Michigan 49501

Unless otherwise stated, Scripture quotations are taken from the Holy
Bible, New International Version, © 1973, 1978, 1984 by the
International Bible Society. Used by permission of Hodder &
Stoughton Ltd. All rights reserved.

The text paper used in this book has been made from wood
independently certified as having come from sustainable forests.

British Library Cataloguing Data
A catalogue record for this book is available from the British Library.

Printed and bound in Reading by Cox & Wyman Ltd.

Dedication

This book is dedicated to:

The children and young people whose words are contained within it and to the millions more just like them throughout Latin America.

All those who have so generously supported the work of Toybox – you are very much part of this story.

God – thank you for your grace and mercy. It is a real privilege to be part of these amazing stories of hope, but all the glory goes to you.

Acknowledgements

Special thanks to the children and young people who helped with this book – your input was incredibly valuable. Thank you for sharing your lives, ideas, thoughts, hopes and dreams and for making this book what it is.

Thanks to all my colleagues at Toybox for their support. Particular thanks to Sally McIver and Andy Stockbridge for their continued encouragement, advice and understanding during this project.

Thanks to Diana Archer for reading the text and for her very helpful feedback and comments which helped me to develop my writing. Thanks to Sarah Shelley and Di Parry for also reading the text and commenting on the content, and to Becky Viccars and Liz Potter for their ongoing support and encouragement.

Thanks to Hannah Heard for helping with the translation of the material contained in this book. Thanks also go to all those in Latin America who assisted with the collection of information and to Richard Hanson for the use of his photos.

Thanks to Chris and Richard Rice, Carol Barwick, Hannah Heard, Gail Murray, Hannah Peters, Georgina Bowyer, Hazel Ireland, Christine Talbot, Jaime Camposeco, Rachael Sandall, Katy Kearns, Harry Lopez and Andy Stockbridge who provided material and ideas for this book.

I am also grateful to Martin Smith, Pete Greig, Nicky Cruz and Mark and Lindsay Melluish for their support of this project.

Finally, I would particularly like to thank the children and young people who have always made me feel so welcome in Latin America. Thanks also to the staff who work in the projects – I have learnt a lot through working with you; your dedication to the children is an inspiration.

Contents

Foreword

We are delighted to have been asked to write the foreword for this book because we are in no doubt that the stories it contains are going to grip and inspire you as you read its pages.

We've had a heart for the work of Toybox for many years both as a church and as a family, one that initially was stirred up by our own children as they were drawn on a daily, or rather hourly basis to the Toybox stall at the New Wine summer conference! We were all very soon hooked and have been excited to see its growth and development over the years.

But then came the opportunity (for Lindsay) to go to Guatemala and actually to meet many of these street children for myself. That trip opened my eyes to things I had never seen before. The extreme poverty was something I had never witnessed in the flesh and I don't think I will ever be the same again. When you meet children – as you will do in this book – who live in cardboard boxes or on a rubbish dump, it changes your perspective for ever.

One day I visited some of the communities in Escuintla, about an hour south of Guatemala City. To walk up 'roads' lined with corrugated iron shacks, each of which was a dwelling, housing a family with several children, was moving to say the least. Children played outside, older ones looking after tinies. With no running water or sanitation it was hard to imagine how families could function in such difficult circumstances. Often they can't, which is why so many children end up on the streets and why Toybox supports teams to go into these communities to try to offer the resources to improve family life. Their work was truly amazing and will undoubtedly lead to many more stories similar to the ones found in the pages of this book.

Later that day, on our way back to the city, we stopped off at an open-air swimming pool where some girls from the Salem home were having a wonderful day out as a treat. They were in and out of the pool, playing games and having a fantastic time. We met Diana who had been rescued from the dangers and poverty which exist in Escuintla, the place we had visited earlier. What a contrast! Diana had arrived malnourished and tiny, having known only a life of abuse and begging prior to being rescued. Now she loves to sing (she sang one song after another that afternoon) and is able to enjoy simply being a child.

She was one of many I met who now live in the homes which Toybox support and, as you will see as you read on, each one is a testimony to the work and also to God himself who is transforming these children into young girls and boys who are not just doing 'OK' but who are blossoming – gorgeous, happy children who are fulfilling the potential He has given them and experiencing something of life in all its fullness. Many of them, I feel sure, will go on to make a significant and valuable contribution to the country which is their home. What a wonderful thing.

We could tell you so much more about the children in Guatemala, but we won't because we'd rather you read on and discover these stories of changed lives and renewed hope told through the eyes and words of the children themselves. We pray that as you do so, you will be moved by the needs that exist in our world and amazed at what our God has done in the lives of these children; our all-powerful, all-loving, life-changing God who not only reaches into and affects the lives of the children in Latin America, but does the same for us too.

May the reminder through these pages of His power to transform and bring hope cause you to take Him deeper into your heart and worship Him more, or to recognise His power and love for the first time.

Lindsay and Mark Melluish
Leaders of St Paul's Church, Ealing and on the
leadership team of New Wine

Preface

Introducing Toybox:
It's not just child's play

Speak up for those who cannot speak for themselves,
for the rights of all who are destitute. Speak up and
judge fairly; defend the rights of the poor and needy.

Proverbs 31:8–9

Angela Murray works for Toybox and the vast majority of the stories she tells come from children she has had the privilege of helping through her work with Toybox partner organisations in Latin America.

Every day, Toybox offers hope and opportunities to hundreds of street children and children at high risk in Latin America, helping them fulfil their dreams. Pioneered in 1992 in response to a BBC Everyman documentary, *'They shoot children, don't they'*, Toybox is a growing response to the injustice faced by street children in Latin America. Based in the UK and funded entirely by voluntary donations, we work in partnership with indigenous organisations to help the people of Latin America offer a future to their children.

We focus our efforts on street children who have no home at all and on those at highest risk. They are

11

survivors of injustice, natural disaster and personal tragedy. Some hope for a hot meal, a shower and some clean clothes. Others hope for a family and a home. For others, the dream is to play for a football team, or to go to school for the first time or to learn a trade. Whatever their dream, Toybox aims to listen to them and make their voices heard. We raise awareness of their plight. We are working to bring their interests to the attention of decision-makers. And we respond to the needs of the children now.

We give them the opportunity to leave the street. We offer practical help, friendship, training, education and homes, as appropriate. We find them and help them when they first become homeless, which is when they are at highest risk. Prevention is better than cure so we tackle root causes of children becoming homeless. Wherever possible we reunite them with caring relatives. We support teams helping children at high risk and their communities – with education, training and social action. This helps prevent children becoming street children.

Relationships are at the heart of everything Toybox does. We treat each child (and supporter) as an individual. We recognise that young people need security so we support long-term projects. For example, in Guatemala we support El Castillo, a comprehensive rescue and rehabilitation programme for street children. This includes a street team, day centre, hostel and six small children's homes with specialist staff. We also support work with some of the most vulnerable children in Cochabamba in Bolivia in partnership with Red Viva and, in addition to this, we are involved in an exciting programme to help street children projects throughout Latin America.

Toybox is based on caring Christian principles but we help all children who need our support, regardless of faith. We seek only to partner projects carried out to the highest standards of care and child protection. We facilitate the sharing of good practice. We help our Latin American partner organisations to become sustainable.

Toybox can be contacted using the details below and more information can be found on our website: www.toybox.org

> Toybox
> PO Box 660,
> Amersham,
> HP6 5YT.
> Tel: 0845 466 0010
> Email: info@toybox.org
> Registered charity number: 1084243

1

Whispers of Hope: Through the eyes of a street child

"This book does not contain little stories, it contains big stories that define the life and character of a child."

Nicky Cruz

"Will you remember me when you go back to England?" Maria asked. Her eyes remained fixed on the ground in front of her and she took another sniff from her bottle of glue. "Of course I will", I replied, "I don't think I'll ever forget you. Besides, I have your photo now, I won't forget you." There was a short pause, then she replied, "No, but will you really remember me? Will you remember me on Christmas Day when you are in your lovely house with your family around you? Will you remember that I am still here, on this rock, on my own, on Christmas Day?" Her voice contained a combination of anger, upset and fear. Though she won't ever know it, I won't ever forget her and her words will always stay with me.

Why street kids?

It was a desire to help children like Maria that first prompted me to travel to Guatemala. While at university I had managed to get myself involved in some work with the homeless. This had been a real eye opener for me and it sparked my interest in issues of poverty and injustice. My concern was fuelled further as I began to read several books on the subject. One in particular had a real effect on me; it told of the street children of Brazil. I started reading it one afternoon and just couldn't stop reading it; it must have been about two in the morning by the time I put it down. A range of emotions were raging within me.

I felt angry at the injustice of our world, shocked by the abuse the children suffered and challenged by the example of those who had given up everything to try to make a difference. The problems seemed overwhelming, but I knew that I wanted to try to play my part in making the world a better place. I looked around for options and the work of Toybox grabbed my attention. Here was an organisation dedicated to doing all it could to give life and hope to street children in Latin America. They were looking for volunteers to join them in their work and I wondered if this could be my chance. A bit more research, an application and an interview later and there it was. I had a place on the Toybox gap year. Come September I would be off to Guatemala.

A world away from home

I don't think anything can truly prepare you for the experience of working with street children. From the outside, it is so easy to think of 'street children' as one big group. Once you start working with them, they become individuals. It is so easy to look at a picture of a street child and to feel sorry for them for a moment, but then to continue on with your life. It is quite something else to actually see where they live and to keep seeing them every day, realising that this is their reality, day in, day out, every week of the year. Video footage and pictures are great at one level; they seem to make the world smaller for us. The problem is, they can't convey the full story.

A picture doesn't allow you to experience what it smells like at the rubbish dump in Zone 3 of Guatemala City; a place that was home to young Francisco and many other children like him. A picture does little to really convey the atmosphere of a place. Only when you stand there does the tension and the darkness really hit you. And even then, it only had to hit me for a limited time. I could go home; these children we were working with could not.

Telling their story

The fact that this book has been written at all is a result of my encounters and experiences with Maria and many others like her in Latin America. These children, the staff and the people of Latin America have challenged me, inspired me, moved me and taught me more than any lecture, sermon or book ever has. They have literally changed my world. They helped me to view things from a whole new perspective. They inspired me to give up my ideas of a career in psychology and to focus my efforts instead on changing things for the better for the poorest of the poor. It is my privilege to be able to write this book, to give these children the opportunity to tell their own stories and to let you see into their world. I won't ever forget them and their desire for a better tomorrow.

As you will see, these children are all unique; they're all different. But, rather than wanting you to feel sorry for them, they simply want to have some of the things which we all take for granted. Some want an education, some a family, some a chance to train in a particular career. For each one, the answers are slightly different. Their ability to rise above the trials and difficulties of life and to hold on to their hopes and dreams despite all that has happened to them is truly inspiring. It is also a real testament to the way that, through the work of Toybox, God has brought and continues to bring transformation to young lives, bringing hope to those places of the world where humanly speaking there can seem to be no hope.

Through the chapters of this book you will meet children like Maria whose life is still hard, whose reality is still a nightmare and who dreams of something better. However, the story does not stop there. You will also meet many children who have moved on from their life on the streets. The changes in them are remarkable, their stories at times are quite simply miraculous.

Representatives of many

Although this book is very much about the children, young people and communities who have contributed to it, it is also about much more than that. These children can be seen as representatives of millions of other children like them throughout Latin America and the world as a whole. I have picked them not because they are any more special than any other children but because I know them. It is my hope and prayer that over the coming years, Toybox may get to know many more children like them as we seek to expand the work that we support in Latin America. The need is real and the opportunities are many.

In the same way, I write this as a representative of the many hundreds and thousands of staff and volunteers across Latin America and the UK who give so much to be part of initiatives like Toybox and the local projects we support in Latin America. When you read this book you will read about a selection of children and about some of my experiences. However, I hope that you will read beyond these words and remember that this story is about more than just those of us who are named here – we speak on behalf of and represent many others.

For ethical and child protection reasons, the names of all the children and young people featured in this book have been changed. In some cases, it was the children who selected the alternative name we would use – they enjoyed choosing a new identity for themselves! Photos have been used to illustrate the stories but these photos do not correspond to the stories presented in this book. Although we would have liked to have kept the names and photos as they were, we value the children too much to do anything which could possibly be detrimental to them or their future life. The bold text in the book helps you see when it is the children or staff members who are speaking. The children's words have been translated from the original Spanish text and every attempt has been made to ensure that it is as close to their original words as possible.

Let the children give to you

Toybox has been hugely blessed, challenged and inspired through its contact with these special children and young people. It is our prayer that their stories will bless, challenge and inspire you in a similar way. It could be that for you, as it was for me, meeting the children in this book, through the words they speak, could literally turn your world around.

Elephants and spiders' webs – Carol Barwick, former staff member of Toybox

It was my first proper day working with the street children in Guatemala. Having waited nine years to meet with and love these children suddenly I was so afraid of how I felt. What if I had nothing to give them? Could I really begin to understand how it felt to have next to nothing – would I even dare?

I looked at this little boy playing with his friend and I froze. Everything people had encouraged me with, every gift I had ever been blessed with dried and shrivelled one by one. I couldn't do this. I had failed before I had even begun.

And then it happened. HE came over to me. This little boy who didn't speak my language and had quite possibly been abused by stranger after stranger came up to me, someone he'd never met before and started to sing.

It was a ridiculous song. The one about elephants walking on a piece of spider web and falling off one by one but I knew it! I linked arms with him and we started to sing; he in Spanish, me in English about these ridiculously huge creatures trying to maintain this colossal task with very little ability and only being able to do it with help – an object lesson perhaps?

We forget that these children have so much to give if only we would allow them to – as you continue to read this book – don't be afraid to let THEM bless YOU.

2

Treasure in the Rubbish: At home in the streets of Latin America

"I have come to realise more and more that the greatest disease and the greatest suffering is to be unwanted, unloved, uncared for, to be shunned by everybody, to be just nobody to no one."

Mother Teresa of Calcutta

In order to fully appreciate the amazing stories of hope contained within this book, it is important to get an understanding of where these children have come from. What has life been like for them in the past, why do these children end up on the streets and what does that really mean?

Life has been bad for me – Maicol, aged 14 years

Life has been bad for me. I don't feel good on the street because I feel cold and it is dangerous. My life is bad because I go around dirty. I don't wash or brush my hair. I don't respect anyone and I have to defend myself from others. I don't like anything of the streets. I want to find a place to sleep, food, love and I want to keep warm. I like to paint on wood. I like it when people take notice of me. I like to eat, sleep and play the game Bancopoly. When I get older I would like to have a house and belong to the army. I want to be a soldier. I was sad at Christmas because my family weren't with me. Anyway it is not happy to be on the streets. If I could change the world, I would change the poverty – so that all of those who don't have a home would have one. I would change enemies for friendship.

Meeting the street kids

The first time I ever met a street child I remember feeling very apprehensive. I was still in my first week in Guatemala and spoke very little Spanish as I was just about to begin my month of Spanish training in a nearby town called Antigua. I was spending the evening with a local street team, who would visit the children on the streets each afternoon and evening. Their aims were to get to know the children, to earn their trust and to try to help them to look at possible options for the future.

We climbed into the minibus and set off to find our first group of children. It was dark and actually a little chilly. The team warned us that we needed to be on our guard as we would be going to some of the most dangerous parts of Guatemala City.

As it turned out, once we arrived at the first port of call for the night, my anxiety soon subsided. I don't know quite what I had expected but I certainly wasn't expecting what happened next. Despite my poor Spanish, from my perspective the evening was a great success. The street team had obviously managed to build up a real rapport with the children and as soon as we arrived they were keen to welcome us and to see what activities might be on offer. As I was introduced as part of the team, the children soon accepted me and took delight in teaching me some new Spanish words. I spent most of the evening sitting on the side of the road, playing snakes and ladders and helping with some colouring-in activities. As I say that, you may be imagining some very young children were taking part, but this was not the case. There are younger children living on the streets, but this was a group of teenagers, mainly boys, who had been on the streets for some time.

Regardless of their age, these boys just loved to play games and to colour in. I guess they had missed out on these things as children and for them this was a chance to play and to forget about the reality of life for a while. I thought about my younger sister back in England who was seventeen at the time. I was fairly sure that if I retuned from Guatemala and presented her with a game of Snakes and Ladders and a colouring book as gifts, she would be less than impressed! However, these kids were really enjoying it and as their characters and personalities began to be revealed, I began to see them as the individual children that they really were.

From the comfort of England it is certainly easy to think of street children as one large group, but the longer you spend with them, the more you begin to see them as individual people. You learn more of their stories and you hear of their hopes and their dreams for the future.

How many are there?

Nobody knows quite how many street children there are in Latin America and estimates vary widely. Many organisations quote a figure of 40 million, but there really is no way of knowing exactly. Street children are very difficult to count as they move around a lot and they are normally not attending school or any other institution that would keep track of them. It is also difficult to obtain accurate statistics, as definitions of street children vary widely. At Toybox, we differentiate between street children (those children who spend most of their days and nights on the street with very little or no family support) and high-risk children (those children in the poorest areas of Latin America who are at high risk of becoming street children in the future).

Why are they there?

There are many reasons why children end up on the streets. For each child the story is different and, as you read the stories in this book, you will have the opportunity of finding out how these particular children came to be on the streets.

Although the factors that lead to street life are different for individual children, there are some common causes which we find when we survey the children. These can be divided into 'push factors' – factors that push children to a life on the streets, and 'pull factors' – factors which make it more likely that children will choose to leave home and take to a life on the streets.

Push factors *include things like:*
- **Natural disasters**
- **Poverty**

- Family breakdown
- Violence in the home
- Abandonment by parents
- Orphans
- Babies born on the streets

Pull factors *include things like:*
- The lure of the freedom of the city
- The search for a better life
- Friends
- Drug addiction

A day in my life – Magdalena, aged 15 years

At 7 o'clock in the morning, with pain and with courage, I wake up and I fold up my blanket as I do each day. My home is the corner of the pavement. I take a little of the water I have saved and I wash my hands and my face. Then I walk about 3km to a restaurant in Zone 1 where I ask for food from the people on the street. I also knock on the window of the coffee shop where people are eating and I ask for a little bit of bread so that I can eat. I am not always successful. Each day I go through this same routine in the hope that I can get enough to satisfy my appetite.

I ask for help, for money, for coins. I use some of the money to buy solvents which I sniff to help me to forget about how hard my life is. Many other street kids want my bottle of solvent and sometimes they fight to take it from me.

I walk the length of the 6th avenue and I come to a shop that sells electrical appliances. I spend many hours at this shop, watching the televisions in the windows until it is dinner time.

Then the night comes and I join a group to go to sleep. There are always horrendous dangers all around me including robbery, rape and death.

My family are OK by me, but my brothers are not. I left home because my brother treated me badly. He hit me. I don't like living on the streets. I started taking drugs because a girl showed me how to. One of the reasons I take solvents is because they help me forget about my mum. She died. I don't want to continue living on the streets. I want to leave and to go to a place like El Castillo (*a local organisation helping street children*). I also want to stop taking drugs. I would like to be a teacher in the future. I would tell the children not to take drugs. I would tell them that life in the street is violent. It is good to live in a home because children who live in homes have friendship and have many things to do. The streets only have drugs and bad things.

The man at the petrol station

Street children are often massively misunderstood by the society which surrounds them, indeed by the world in general. They are often depicted as criminals, as worthless and as an embarrassment to their cities and their countries. This is something the children are well aware of and it is something that only adds to their already mounting problems.

People hit me and they discriminate against me. I suffer abuse from the authorities.

Jasmine, aged 16 years

The police are violent towards us; they think that we should be living in houses.

Anna, aged 15 years

During one of my overseas trips, something happened which drew my attention to the extent of the hatred which exists amongst some members of society. The local organisation I was with was trying to find ways of getting local people and local businesses to support its work. The team obviously do a large number of miles each week in their minibuses, driving to the various street groups and ferrying other children to and from the children's homes. For this reason, they decided to approach a local garage to ask whether they might consider giving free or discounted petrol to the charity. The owner of the garage came out to speak to the team. He listened to what they had to say and then said, with complete seriousness and with a look of disgust on his face, that the petrol station would gladly provide free petrol but only if we promised to use it to burn the children.

Thankfully there are many people in Latin America who don't share the views of this petrol station owner and who are dedicating themselves to working for the poor. However, it does illustrate the misunderstandings which there are about the children, and the levels of anger and violence that they experience during their time on the streets.

I don't find happiness here – Jose, aged 13 years

The street has given me nothing good. Because of this my life has been sad. There are people who don't

love me and treat me as though I was a dog and I get sad. The police beat me and take away my money that I collect during the day. I sell sweets on the streets and on the buses and with this money I eat and buy glue. Today on the street I realise that I don't find happiness here. I've only found sadness and pain.

The rubbish dump

Working with the street children at the rubbish dump was the part of the work that affected me the most. It was there that I met boys like Francisco, aged 11, who very rarely left the rubbish dump. At one level he seemed like he was 11 going on 40 – he was so responsible and so worldly-wise for one so young. At another level, he was just an ordinary 11-year-old boy who loved to play, liked to be cheeky and who never seemed to run out of energy!

The rubbish dump in Zone 3 of Guatemala City is huge, unlike anything I have ever seen before. Several hundred people live on and around the dump either in tin shack houses or simply sleeping on some cardboard or whatever it is they can lay their hands on that day. The rubbish dump may seem a strange place to live. If you or I suddenly became homeless, I guess our first thought wouldn't be 'Quick, where's my nearest rubbish dump?' However, the reason they choose the dump is because it is an incredibly resourceful place to live. The children and adults spend their days searching the rubbish for leftover food and for anything of value that they could sell on to other people. As you can imagine, the kids at the dump are frequently ill and they are at risk from cuts and infections which they pick up as they scour the rubbish day in and day out.

As a new rubbish truck approaches the dump, people gather to try to be the first to get a chance to get a look and to take out things of value. This is especially the case when they know that the truck has come in from Zone 10 or one of the other 'richer' areas of Guatemala City. This really is a case of the poor having to live off the scraps of the rich. To make things worse, up on the hillside, just above the side of the dump, a 'viewing area' has been constructed so that tourists and interested observers can sit and watch as the poor search the rubbish. I wonder how many people, from different nations of the world, have gone home with photos of Francisco and his friends, taken from that viewing point.

I spent many hours with Francisco, often doing very basic things such as playing a game of marbles in the dirt by the side of the dump. At the end of the day, when I got back to the flat where I was staying, I was so keen to have a shower and to get changed. The smell of the dump could be overwhelming. The longer I worked with the street team, the harder I found it to do the work. In the beginning these children were children I didn't know. It was hard to see the conditions they lived in but in some ways it could be easy to distance myself from it. The more I got to know them, the more it began to hit home. These children became like friends and more than anything I wanted things to change for them. At the end of each day I could go home but they couldn't. And the next day, when I returned, there they were, still on the rubbish dump, still hungry, still searching for food, still no nearer to a better or safer future... and still just children.

You live sad – Jerson, approximately 14 years old

Life on the streets is very difficult. You suffer a lot. You live sad. They've hit me. I've been hungry and cold. I've hit some other people; I've fought in the street. It's all very difficult. Most of all, I feel lonely. They humiliate me and I am far from my family.

Dreams of a better tomorrow

Despite the things that have happened to them in the past and the difficulties of their current lives, it is important that these children are not simply seen as 'victims'. Taking to the streets is never an easy option but it can be a survival strategy when life at home becomes intolerable. The words of one young boy stick in my mind. I don't remember his name but I recall him saying, "The streets aren't so bad; not as bad as people say. Living on the streets is a lot easier and a whole lot less dangerous than it was back home".

Once they are on the streets, these children show incredible resilience. Not only are they able to survive by their wits, they also tend to form themselves into groups and demonstrate an amazing amount of care for the other members of the group. Although in the beginning I had a fear of working with the street children, I soon began to realise that if anything was to happen when we were out, it would be the kids themselves who would be the first to step in and help me.

Life is hard for these kids. They often become addicted to drugs and many get into trouble with the law. But they are also just normal children with hopes and dreams for the future. They are people with rights and, given the right opportunities, they have incredible potential for the future.

I would like to be happy in a house with a family. I like to play football a lot, especially as a goalkeeper. I like to be able to draw and paint. In the future I would like to study and to work and have a happy family.

Felix, aged 13 years

In the future I would like to the president.

Ramiro, aged 16 years

I want to be an obedient boy, I want to behave well. I would like to work, to help my grandfather. I don't want to be disobedient anymore. I don't want to try drugs.

Carlos, aged 11 years

I like to do crafts, draw and paint. In the future I would like to work painting pictures and be an inventor and do experiments.

Juan, aged 12 years

Unfortunately, helping these children to achieve their dreams and to fulfil their potential is not an easy process. There are many obstacles for them to overcome and for some it can just seem to be too difficult. Despite his attempts to leave behind his life on the streets, Francisco has so far failed to successfully complete any programme which he has started and, seven years on, is still on the streets. However, with the right support and opportunities, some of these children are able to choose a different future for themselves, as you will see later in this book.

Working with the street team was the ultimate challenge to the materialistic culture which I come from.

It is a challenging vocation requiring lots of patience, determination and love. Working on the streets you will face many setbacks and disappointments, but you know it is worth it for every child you are able to help.

This chapter closes with the words of a song, 'Don't judge me', written at a special workshop for street children in Guatemala. Their challenge to us is not to see them as they are now, but to help them to be what they could be in the future.

> *What will happen with my future?*
> *What will happen with my country?*
> *I don't know if I'll reach my youth*
> *Or be just another story.*
> *I dream of a different world, I ask myself if it*
> *will come*
> *If you would think about me today, maybe it*
> *could become a reality.*
>
> *Today I talk to you about what I have*
> *suffered*
> *Of those who always deny good things.*
> *It wasn't our fault that we were born.*
> *Don't judge me for being a child of the street.*
> *I never chose my future.*
> *And, you are happy – you have a home.*
>
> *I dream of a different world, I ask myself if it*
> *will come*
> *If you would think about me today, maybe it*
> *could become a reality.*

Today my future is in your hands, part of me is in you.
If you would think about me today, it could become a reality.

3

Living at High Risk:
The cycle of poverty and abuse

"But I, being poor, have only my dreams. I have spread my dreams under your feet; tread softly, because you tread on my dreams."

William Butler

I fully expected adapting to life in Latin America to be a challenge. Aware of the numerous issues I would need to deal with, I tried to think through what life would be like and how I would be able to adjust to all I would see and experience. Looking back, I know that the time I invested in preparing to go was well worth it – it certainly made adapting easier. One thing I didn't do though, was to really prepare myself for coming back to the UK once my placement was over; I really didn't think I would need to. I had lived in England all my life; surely it would be straightforward to return after my relatively short time somewhere else. Interestingly, I found the transition back to life in the UK much harder than that original adaptation to life in Latin America had ever been.

Culture is a very interesting concept. People are people the world over but at the same time there can be a world of difference between the ways that things function in different societies. The affluence of the UK was something I very much took for granted before I travelled elsewhere. Coming home from my first overseas placement, it was this that hit me the hardest and this I struggled with most. It probably didn't help that I returned to the UK at Christmas time when extravagance and materialism tends to be at its highest. I recall standing in a large supermarket looking at the numerous shampoos on sale. The vast choice seemed overwhelming and for some reason the act of choosing one took far longer than it should have done! During the same visit, I was struck by the amount of food that people were buying. We were now into the school holidays and the majority of people were shopping with their children, many of whom I heard pleading with their parents for extra items to be put into the trolleys. As I looked around at the faces of the shoppers and their children, and as "Winter Wonderland" played in the background over the shop PA system, my mind wandered back to think of the faces of the people I had met in some of the poorest communities of Guatemala. It seemed as if they were from two different worlds, not just two different countries. It was so hard to see what they could have in common. On the surface, those people I was watching in the UK appeared to have everything. They were buying more food than they needed, they drove to the supermarket in a car, I assume that they lived in a house and that those children following them around normally attended school and had numerous sets of clothes stuffed into their wardrobes at home. Those faces I thought of in Guatemala represented a whole different way of life. For many, home was little more than a shack, often home-made and often less than waterproof. Many of their children were not in school and often lacked basic items such as shoes. Food was a less than reliable commodity and luxuries such as running water and electricity were only available to the fortunate few. However, as I thought about those two groups, I wondered which one was happier – those who had more or those who, at least materially, seemed to have less.

Working with the poorer communities was filled with daily challenges. Perhaps one of the hardest was the very real personal challenge to the ideas and behaviours which I took as normal from my childhood in England. One of the things that really hit me was the gratefulness which many of the people showed for the things that they had and for each and every small gift they received. What a contrast to the culture of the West, where there is such drive to want more and better 'stuff' – all in the quest to be happy. Does it really make us happy?

Some of the people I met in the shanty towns seemed to have an inner happiness that I rarely saw in England. When I visited they were so keen to invite me in. They would give us the best that they had in terms of drink and food. This might have been just a tortilla or some rice but to families such as these that could be a lot. They were welcoming, accepting and the smiles they gave us revealed such an inner joy. They never seemed too busy, too stressed or too preoccupied to speak to us. Guatemala is a predominantly Christian country and many of those we worked with had a really strong faith in God. They seemed able to trust Him despite their circumstances and accepted the difficulties of life in a way that seemed a huge contrast from the culture of the UK, where we strive so hard to have as easy a life and as nice a home as possible.

Introducing Katarin

Although I never want to forget those personal challenges, the smiling faces of the people, the unconditional welcome we received and the depth of their faith in God, there is more to tell about these communities. Despite the ability of many to cope with life as it was, many of those we met and worked with did dream of a better tomorrow. A tomorrow in which their children could go to school. A tomorrow with more security. A tomorrow in which food wouldn't be a problem. A tomorrow with running water and electricity. A tomorrow which just seemed a little bit fairer.

In addition, there were also those who just couldn't get to grips with life as it was. They couldn't cope with their children, the lack of security, the fear of natural disasters and crime, and the lack of hope for the future. It was typically the children of these families with whom we found ourselves working. Children like Katarin.

Katarin was about 3 or 4 years of age when the team first started to work with her during their visits to her hometown, Escuintla, located about an hour south of Guatemala City. The environment is hot and humid, the atmosphere intense, and a smell of danger and corruption fills the air. The people there have 'houses' that provide shelter, but these are essentially an umbrella of tin over a dirt floor. The poverty and deprivation are undeniable.

Katarin's street seemed to be the epitome of what Escuintla stood for. It is an area well known for prostitution and drug crime and is characterised by gangs. Men clearly under the influence of alcohol or drugs hang around; on certain days it wouldn't be unusual to see a couple of them passed out on the ground. It also wouldn't be unusual to see scantily clad women sitting or standing in doorways.

Katarin's doorway was often empty. There were occasions when the team would hear a baby crying, but the increasing volume made no difference. There was no one in and no one would come running to see what the problem was. The team would often find 4-year-old Katarin wandering around the streets alone. Raggedly dressed in a vest and a pair of shorts, both covered in dirt and with no shoes on her feet, she looked utterly hopeless. Many of the children we worked with seemed unbelievably strong and managed to laugh and play despite all the odds. Katarin, however, had no idea how to play. She had no idea how to communicate with others, and she had no idea how to look after herself. On several occasions the team had to stop her from running out in front of oncoming cars.

Her mother was probably brought up in a similar situation. She wasn't able to care for herself let alone her children. Sometimes when the team went round, Katarin would be with her uncle, but that was never reassuring, as he was heavily involved in drugs. Her situation was desperate.

The cycle of poverty and abuse

The good news for Katarin is that she is one of the children who have been helped by a Toybox-supported team and she now has a new chance in life, which she is enjoying within the safety of a small home run by a Christian couple from Guatemala. However, the team's experiences with Katarin in Escuintla could really be from any country in Latin America, where millions of children just like her are growing up in desperate situations on the outskirts of many of the major cities. By understanding more about the living conditions in these places and the challenges that many face, we can begin to see how the cycle of poverty and abuse continues from one generation to another. Children are often left to survive rather than being given the opportunity to thrive. As they in turn grow up and have children, they typically lack parenting skills and have missed out on an education themselves, and so the problems continue.

One young lady we have had contact with in recent times is Jennifer. Now nearly 18 years of age, Jennifer has taken the time to tell us her own story. Her words give us a real insight into the reality of what life can be like for these children and the very real consequences this can have not just on their childhood and teenage years, but well into adult life too. Jennifer was born in El Salvador on 20th March 1988. Her mum gave birth to her outside of her shack and was shocked when eventually the labour was over and she looked down to see Jennifer lying in the mud. Jennifer tells us what happened next:

Growing up – the early years

My mum never gave me any attention, even from when I was little. My father always said I was the daughter of another person. Then, one day, he simply left.

Then, another day, my mum went out and left me with my grandmother. When she came back she brought another man home with her called Edwin. He built a house for us but my grandmother didn't like him because he was in a gang of thieves. On many occasions my mum hit me really hard. She said that I had lost money but what she didn't know was that it was Edwin who had stolen it.

A life of crime

When I was 3 and a half, Edwin died of a brain haemorrhage; he was only 28 years old. We left that place and my mum got caught driving a car that was stolen. She was sent to prison for four years. I used to go to visit my mum in prison with my grandmother and my cousins. During this time we all had to sleep in a small room – it was so very cramped. My aunts had to earn money to keep us. They said they worked in a restaurant but in reality they were working in a strip club.

Carlos – the new man on the scene

My mum was only in prison for two years; she was let out early for good behaviour. I was 5 years old when she came out of prison. After she left prison, my mum fell in love with another guy by the name of Carlos. We all lived together, Carlos, my mum and me in the country of Guatemala. However, he had other women.

We had to move from where we were living to a house made of wood as there were too many problems with a lady there who had tried to beat my mum with a machete various times.

My stepfather would also beat my mum constantly with his hand. One time he tried to drown her in a barrel full of water. I was scared and at times we had to run away and sleep in the houses of different neighbours. He used to come home drugged up and liked to burn things.

When I was 6 years old he called me and touched all my body. I told my mum but she didn't believe me because she said I was the one who provoked it. He raped me when I was 7 years old. He put rags in my mouth so I wouldn't shout.

When my little sister Carlita was about to be born, he said that a rat was going to be born.

Returning to El Salvador

One day my stepfather hit me with a pipe and left me with marks on my back – I was severely bruised. I took a dark red suitcase and borrowed Q50 (about £3.50). I returned to El Salvador alone. I was just 9 years old. It was night-time when I got there. I was crying and some men took me to the home of one of my aunts. One man tried to rape me but he couldn't.

I left my aunt's house and went to my grandmother's house. Soon my mum arrived; she was looking for me. My grandmother was suspicious that something bad was happening to me and took me to the doctor for an examination. It was then they realised that I had been raped by Carlos, my stepfather. I didn't like being in my grandmother's house because I had to do all the housework. I lived with her for two years.

When I was 11 years old I saw my mum again and she had another little baby called Yulma. She said she was going to burn her because she was HIV positive. Of course my mum was also HIV positive and in the end she was confined to a hospital in Guatemala because the situation was hopeless. My little sister was also becoming increasingly unwell and her hair was falling out bit by bit.

After a month, my mum was able to come out of the hospital. At that time they did the HIV test on me too and four years ago I found out that I was also HIV positive.

Turning 15

On my fifteenth birthday we celebrated in a tin shed. My family made me a cake and we had lunch together. Three days later my mum went back into hospital because her illness had got worse and she was really bad. I had to sell my body to a man who lived nearby so that he would give me the money I needed to be able to travel to see my mum in the hospital. My mum died one Saturday at 7 in the morning.

After my mum's death, I went with some friends to another place and I started working in strip clubs where I earned Q,1000 (about £75) a week for dancing semi nude and selling my body. I worked there for a year and a half. There were many times when I felt sick. I also felt angry about doing things like this. It was like I was in prison as the people I worked for put four padlocks on my door. In the end I escaped by taking off some boards and leaving through a window.

I returned to where I used to work and I got a job

in a restaurant as a waitress. There I made friends with some young people who sold drugs. They offered me some and I tried it. That night I was so drugged. They all abused me. I was completely disappointed and heartbroken and tried to commit suicide by cutting my veins. Somehow I survived.

Moving on a couple of years, Jennifer is slowly starting to put her life back together again. She wanted to tell her story as a warning to other young people and as an encouragement too. She ends her testimony with the following statement:

A decision to change

I am now 17 years old and I will soon be 18. I have been through many things that I really wouldn't like to live through again. Life has taught me many good things and many bad things.

I have decided to change. I have some friends who have helped me a lot. I have visited a church. I know that I have done lots of bad things but I really want to be different. I believe that only God can change my life.

I know that my illness won't go away but He can make me a clean woman and I want to achieve that. I wouldn't like the things that have happened to me to happen to other people. That is why I recommend to other girls that if anything similar is happening to you, you should tell someone. Don't be afraid because if not, you could end up like me.

When the streets are safer than 'home'

Life for street children is incredibly difficult and traumatic. However, as Jennifer's story shows, sometimes it can seem like the better option when life at home becomes so difficult. This is why working in the poorest communities is so important. Prevention is better than cure. That's why Toybox supports organisations working in poorer communities to help break the cycle of poverty and abuse. This requires teams dedicated to tackling a whole range of issues, from parenting to social care. Millions of children desperately need help, support and opportunities. By working in this way, we can help to reduce the factors that are likely to lead to children having to leave home and take to the streets.

A desire to learn

Education, among other things, plays a vital role in helping children to break the cycle of poverty and abuse, which is so evident amongst the poor. But getting an education isn't always easy.

In Guatemala the academic year runs from January through to October with school enrolments coming hot on the heels of the New Year celebrations. Although a 'state education' system does exist, this system poses some serious problems for many of the poorer communities. The first problem they face is the distinct lack of schools in poorer areas. For example, one lady got up at 1am to start queuing in order to be able to enrol her son, Frederick, into the only local state secondary school for her area. Those who slept in until 3am missed out. Equally, many elementary children find themselves excluded once enrolments make class sizes rise past fifty-five. Enrolment is necessary every year and there is often no reservation of places for children who have been there the previous year.

Even if parents make it to the front of the queue, they are often asked to pay an enrolment fee that may be as high as £20 (which is the equivalent of about two weeks' wages for many of these people). In addition to this, parents need to kit their kids out with all that is needed. This typically includes the school uniform, physical education kit and school equipment. School equipment isn't usually limited to your typical pencil, pen, ruler and eraser. It often stretches to other items such as dictionaries, card, paper, plasticine and, in some cases, even whiteboard markers for the teacher. We have known of cases where, if a child has failed to turn up with a required item one day (for example, a paintbrush for the art class) then they are turned away for the entire day.

As you can imagine, this all makes for an interesting challenge for a family with five children and a weekly wage equivalent to £10. As a result, many children have very little educational input, if any at all. At this stage, their only hope is that a voluntary, non-governmental agency will step in and either help get the child enrolled into a state-run school or provide some kind of alternative education.

Before I ever travelled to Latin America, I spent some time working in schools within the UK. Although this was good preparation, being involved in education with the kids from the shanty towns was a whole new experience!

Where possible and appropriate, the local team I was with helped families to get kids into state schooling. This involved not only helping the parents to negotiate and understand the system, but also financial support. In many cases this was needed not just to pay for all the required items mentioned above, but also to compensate for the loss of income to the family. Instead of attending school, many children, even very young children, spent their days working. This could include a variety of things such as selling items, shining shoes, begging, washing cars and running errands. This work not only got them out from under their parents' feet, it also brought in vital income which the families often couldn't do without. In our monetary terms, the amounts earned per day were incredibly small but they meant so much to the survival of these families.

Where state schooling wasn't possible for whatever reason, some children were able to attend alternative Toybox-supported schooling. Even those who were able to return to state schooling often required extra help and support and could choose to attend some extra lessons with us in the afternoons.

The charity schools often took place in borrowed buildings or rented accommodation, or occasionally we simply set out some tables and chairs in an area of the community. The children knew when the schools would be happening and would often turn up well in advance of the time school started. It was lovely to see how keen they were to learn and how excited they were that school was about to start. Although some of the children I worked with in England enjoyed at least some of their school lessons, I don't think I ever saw quite such excitement as I witnessed from these children. For many, going to school is something they have always wanted to do, and the time they spend in school is the most positive part of their lives.

Maria, aged 12 years

My life is sad, because when my mum comes home she hits me with a cable and treats me badly. She tells me to do one thing, then after that she tells me to do something else. I've never been bought new clothes for Christmas, (which is the custom here) or even been given any gift. The best thing for me is that I can now go to school to study. The teachers teach me how to read and write, as I have never studied before. In the future I'd like to be a teacher. I want to help children to study so they can learn how to read and write.

Many of the children are obviously a long way behind in their schooling and it isn't uncommon for staff to be doing very basic literacy and numeracy exercises with teenagers. However, despite the obstacles against them, many are keen to work hard to try to achieve a better future for themselves.

Anna, aged 9 years

In the future I want to work as a doctor or teacher. I want to help other children in the way that I have been helped in my studying. I want to study hard to have a happy life with my children.

Sophia, aged 11 years

My life has been sad because most of the time I have

been sick. My brother sometimes treats me badly. I've always lived along the train line. The thing I do most is to go out to sell rellenitos (typical sweets) with my sister. We do this to help my mum. Now my life is better because my house is a bit cleaner. I'm happy because an organisation has come along and helped my mum. They helped us have our own selling business. I am also able to go to school. What I find difficult is doing maths homework because sometimes I don't understand it and no one can help me to do it. What I like most is to go to my neighbours and play with dolls, because in my house I don't have any. In the future I would like to grow up, help my mum when she is an old lady and have a house. I would like to be a teacher to be able to teach the children so that their lives will be better and they can stay away from drugs.

Education is vital to breaking the cycle of poverty and abuse but it can only ever be one part of the solution. The complexity of the issues faced by these families cannot be underestimated. However, the determination and courage shown by children like Jennifer, Anna, Maria and Sophia encourages us to help these families and communities in the best ways we can.

4

The Family Approach

"Feelings of worth can flourish only in an atmosphere
where individual differences are appreciated, mistakes
are tolerated, communication is open, and rules are
flexible – the kind of atmosphere that is found in a
nurturing family."

Virginia Star

Over the past 15 years, Toybox has become increasingly
aware of the importance of working not only with
children, but also with their families and their
communities too. Education forms one part of this work
but other types of family support, therapy and
intervention are also vital for long-term, sustainable
changes to occur.

To help illustrate why a holistic approach is so
important, let me introduce you to a lady called Estrella.
Estrella and her family represent very aptly the real and
heartbreaking situations which some of these families
find themselves in. When I first met families like
Estrella's, I found it hard to believe that significant
changes could happen. The issues were many, the

situations aggressive, complex and difficult and the resources limited.

As you will see, Estrella's early life was anything but easy. However, despite the massive challenges she has faced, Estrella has, with appropriate and consistent support, been able to turn her own life around. The changes that she has made have also meant that her own children now have a much brighter hope for the future. She really is trying in her own way to break the cycle of poverty and abuse.

Introducing Estrella

My name is Estrella. I live in Zone 6 and I want to share something of my life story with all those who wish to read it.

I was born on 31 May 1972. When I was little I remember that my mum had to work hard to feed me and my four siblings. Because she had had no education, all she could do was make tortillas and sell clothes from time to time. My sisters and I would get up at 4am each day in order to fill the public washing area with water. When we had finished we would be given some tortillas with salt on them as our reward.

My dad, my uncle and cancer

My dad did not look after us at all and life was very hard. One day my uncle arrived. My dad started saying that my uncle had only come back to get my mum pregnant and in fact that is what happened. My mum became pregnant with my youngest brother and my dad left.

When my brother was born they detected cancer in my mum's womb and she had to go into hospital. My uncle was left to look after all of us, including our brand new baby brother. He gave us food, washed our clothes and did everything he could for my mum. She was in hospital for about a year and my uncle had to sell a large piece of land in order to pay for her medicine. When my dad found out about her illness, he didn't think that she would survive. He decided he wanted to sell all of us, his children, to some people in the city. Thanks be to God, when he arrived to take us away, my uncle was there and he wouldn't let him take us. My uncle never gave up and he was always there for us.

My mum was now much better and she didn't have to stay in hospital much longer, which was a lovely surprise and a great comfort for us. Soon after she came home, my uncle fell ill and so he and my mum swapped roles, with my mum looking after him instead. During this time he put the paperwork for the house in my mum's name. He had been ill for about two months when he said that he had something to say to me. For some reason though, every time he was about to say it he would just stop and say he was sorry, he just couldn't say it. He hugged me and kissed me instead – he was loving towards all my brothers and sisters but especially to me.

I will never forget the day he died. On that day he could not speak well but suddenly he said in a loud voice, "Sweetheart, bring me a glass of water". When I came back with the water, he drank it then put his hand on my face, rolled over and died. With his death, our future died too because from that time on our mum was in torment. We all had to start working – well, that is all of us except the oldest, who was ill because he had been hit by a motorcycle when he was out begging for money for food.

My dad returns

The worst thing was that my dad returned home and started treating everybody, especially me, very badly. He said that I was not his daughter because I was very thin and that I didn't put on weight because I was such a bad girl. He used loads of very bad words. During this time, my mum had to leave to find work and was away for about two weeks. My dad used this time to abuse me and said that if I told anyone he would kill me. I told my mum but she didn't believe me until the day that she awoke to see my dad crawling towards my bed. I also told the wife of my dad's cousin and they told me that when my mum was away, I should stay with them. I was going through a very difficult time in my life including the fact that my mum was changing in her manner towards me because I was the ugliest of all the sisters and she preferred my other sisters. Sometimes I saw my mum and my sister going out with men and I saw them having intimate relations with them. Perhaps my mum did it from necessity but my sister? I didn't understand.

After a while they started treating me a bit better. My mum found me some work, although she made me give all my money to her. My sister got pregnant and they started splitting the money I earned between the two of them. My dad continued abusing me and when he found that I didn't gratify

him any more, he shouted at me and said that I
would never find a husband. You cannot even start
to imagine how desperate I felt. Then my sister said
that she would leave home if I didn't. So my mum
came to me and told me to leave. So, I collected up
what little I had and left home and went to stay with
my dad's cousin.

Meeting Raul

During this time I often thought about killing myself
and I went to see a friend who could get me some
poison but she refused to give it to me. After a while
I went to the city to work and it was there that I
started to drink and to go out to discos. The worst
thing was that I fell in love with a man who played
with my feelings. He told me that he loved me and
wanted to be with me. He said that he had already
spoken to his parents about it. He had me in a hotel
for three days and then he left me. I was thrown out
onto the street. My life started to get worse.

Within a few months I got to know the man who
is now my partner – Raul. I was not in love with him
but I clung onto him in despair. He is twelve years
older than me and I knew that. I thought that life
could only be better with him but I had no idea what
kind of man he was – he was a drunkard, chauvinist
and all the rest of it. After only a month he started
hitting me, which started bringing back memories of
the treatment that I had received from my dad. My
heart burnt with hatred for my dad and for Raul.

As time went by, he hit me harder and more
frequently. He was drunk more often than not and he
stopped giving me money. There was now a child on

the way but my in-laws had no interest in it, and even less in me. He spent Christmas and New Year drunk, while I spent it crying in our room.

The arrival of Eddy

Time passed and our son was born (Eddy). I thought that Raul would change but things only got worse. When Eddy was only six months old, I found that I was pregnant again. At this point we had nowhere to live so we went to live with his parents. Each day I had to wait until they had finished washing and cooking before I could use the facilities. Time was passing and I was well into my pregnancy. Raul was given the chance of some work selling things in the street but he did not make very much. We also started having problems with his family and, just two weeks before the birth of our child, they threw us out of the house. We went to my mum's house but she insisted that we had to feed all my brothers and sisters as well. That's quite a lot of people and so the money soon ran out.

We tried to find ourselves an apartment to buy but ended up in a hostel. That same day I ended up in hospital and God gave me a baby girl, Mauda.

We eventually returned to my mum's house. She would not help me at all – she wouldn't help wash nappies or even bring me a cup of hot water. We had no money and no job. We decided to try to return to Raul's family. A cousin saw how we had been burgled and said that she had a shack in a shanty town that had been robbed and that we could use it on the condition that we looked after the old lady who lived there. She was an invalid and it was I who ended up looking after her. We didn't have a centavo (Guatemalan coin) between us but there was a box there with beautiful aprons which belonged to the old lady. We sold them and from this we were able to eat. Raul started working selling things on the streets and we became a little more established. But he kept on hitting me because he said that I had lovers – he was wrong.

Desperate for a place of our own

Everything was almost going well when suddenly Raul's family said that they were going to sell the shack. Raul went to speak to his mum but she did not want to help. We spoke to a friend but he could not help either. Every night I ended up sleeping in a car with my two children – my daughter and I on the floor with a bit of cardboard and no sheets. In time, a kind man gave us space in a hostel. We had to sleep on the dirt floor but at least we were altogether.

At this time I was pregnant with my third child and we were trying so hard to find a place of our own. At last we found some land and started living there with just a piece of corrugated iron and some plastic for a roof. Our son, Carlos, was born there and Raul continued beating me. He continued drinking and I hated him so much, just as I hated my dad. I was so full of hate and despair that I started treating our children the way that my mum had treated me. I remember once that Mauda scorched a bit of cloth while she was doing the ironing. I tied her to the bed and beat her relentlessly. Another time, Carlos wet his bed in the night and I got him out of bed and plunged him into some very cold water. Time passed and I became pregnant with our fourth child who was a little girl, Carla.

Life and death

During this time Raul drank continuously for three months and things got worse and worse. I became pregnant with our fifth child. When the time came for his birth, Raul was spending very little time with us – he spent most of each day in bars and when he came home he would hit me in the face and all over my body. He would also hit the children. One day, when our baby boy was only ten months old, he hit him hard. He died of a ruptured spleen. In my heart, I believed it was my fault. I had not really wanted the baby and sometimes I had thought about giving it away.

At about this time my dad died, but I did not go to either his wake or his funeral. As well, at about the time that my baby died, I give thanks to God that we met a team supported by Toybox which works with street children and children in high risk and from dysfunctional homes. They were very interested in my case and started to help me.

The doctors detected that Eddy had a heart murmur. We had no money to pay for treatment, but, thanks to many people with great hearts who sent donations, our son is now healthy. After this our oldest daughter, Mauda, had problems with her sight but again they helped us materially and spiritually.

However, I continued with the same hate for my dad and for Raul and I blamed God for allowing my uncle to die. Although he wasn't my dad, I believed that all that I had gone through would not have happened if my uncle was still alive. I tried various times to kill myself – it was as if my home and my children were not important to me. I wrote a letter where I asked the charity to take my children into their care. I also swore to myself that I would pay back my husband for killing our son.

At this time, thanks to the charity, I had been studying nursing. But, at the end of each day, I would go out with my nursing friends and I got into some very bad stuff. I started becoming unfaithful, getting into adultery, sex and alcohol. Despite all of this, the team carried on helping me with visits from a psychologist and with Bible studies. But nothing changed in my life.

From desperation to depravity

Once I had started working, Raul would always take my pay from me and I would have nothing left. He would go out drinking while I would be looking for extra jobs like washing people's clothes. At one point I got so desperate that I started selling myself for sex. I ended up pregnant with another man's child and had an abortion.

I realise now how much all this was affecting the children. Because they knew that I wanted to kill myself, both Mauda and Carla told other people that they would kill themselves too if I died because they couldn't bear to live with their dad alone. One day we found Eddy selling drugs – he said that he was trying to make some money so that we could eat. It was about this time that things got worse (if that's possible). I found out that the uncle who had loved me and had died was actually my real dad. I started to hate my mum because she hadn't told me earlier. My uncle had been the best person I had known and I still miss him and remember him as if it had been yesterday.

Turning my life around

Praise God that He came into my life at a time when I felt that there was no solution. I met a couple who have been helping me ever since. They sent me to a weekend retreat. It was there that all my pain, hate and sadness disappeared. It was there that I received the hug of a dad and the love of a mum.

I am now a leader in my church, thankful for everything that God has done in my life. Since I gave my life to Him, He has blessed us with a house made of blocks, our children are doing well at school and Raul is drinking less and working more. I pray to God that He will take me to the nations to preach His word and one of my dreams is to go to England to give my testimony in person. I also want to marry Raul – now that I know God, I am able to forgive Raul and I pray that he will forgive me. I pray that together we can see our children grow. We have suffered together and now we are going to be happy together.

To anyone who is reading this, men and women, I beg you that you do not do the things that I have done. Remember that the devil comes to steal, to kill and to destroy. But God came to give you not only life, but life in abundance.

The couple that Estrella refers to, Richard and Chris Rice, recently wrote to me and this is what they had to say about Estrella and her family:

Defining transformation

We would have never dreamt that the same joyful lady who greets us on our visits to her house is the same gloomy, sad lady that we first saw sitting in the corner of the room where we were holding an activity for mums in Santa Faz two years ago.

Nor that the bouncy teenager is the same girl, Mauda, whose notebook we found a year and half ago in which she had written that she thought she had the worst life in the world and that if her mum killed herself she would do likewise because she couldn't bear to live without her.

Nor that the smiling man who greets us with a strong shake of the hand and a huge welcome into his new block-built house is the same man that threw a cloud of terror over the family.

If ever there was a definition of the word transformation, this family is it. It has been a total privilege to watch this family turn from tears to happiness and an even greater privilege to count them as some of our best friends here in Guatemala.

Reuniting children with their families

Taking a family-based approach is vital when working with high-risk children such as Estrella's. It is also an important part of work with the street children. It is sometimes possible for organisations to reunite street children with their families. Obviously, this has to be arranged carefully and with support. Every possible step needs to be taken to ensure that the child is not being returned to a dangerous or abusive situation which they will no doubt run away from at the earliest possible instance. However, there are occasions when the children really want to go home and want to be assisted to do so.

Sometimes it is not possible for street children to go home straight from the streets. There needs to be a process that involves helping both the child and the family. This was the case with a boy called Giovani. I first met Giovani in 1999 when I was working in Guatemala. He had recently left the streets and moved into one of the charity homes for younger boys. In 2000, I met him again during a visit he made to England and Scotland. Over a period of two weeks, Giovani and another boy from a different home spent time with Toybox in the UK. During the trip, Giovani visited my dad's house in the south of Scotland. As a gift, my dad gave both boys a woollen Carlisle United hat (my home town football team)! As well as serving as a reminder of their trip, the hats also kept the boys warm in the slightly chilly British weather. During a trip to Guatemala five years later, in January 2005, I met Giovani again. One of the first things he said to me was "How is your dad?" This was quickly followed by "I still have my Carlisle hat – I wear it sometimes in the evening when it is cold!" I was amazed by his memory but also by the value he attached to the gifts he had been given.

I have heard Giovani described by others as the 'kindly chief'. When he lived in the boys' home it was amazing to see the way that the younger boys would look up to him and obey him. He did not force their respect or obedience; he always treated the boys with firm love and

At home in the streets of Latin America

Breaking the cycle of poverty and abuse

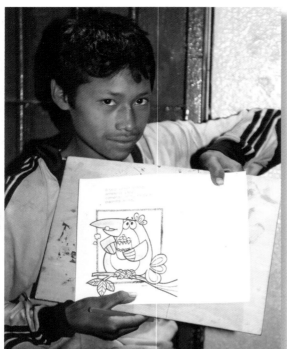

Street art

The pavement for a pillow – trying to get some sleep on the streets of Latin America

Living off the scraps of the rich

Toybox is taking hope to the streets

Me, my house and my chicken

Not your average playground

Waiting for the classroom to open

From humble beginnings

New life, new hope

Someone to notice me – a glimmer of hope

Moving on step by step

Me and my teddy bear

A whole bed just for me

Free to play – the chance
to be children

Our Father who art in heaven

Me and my street family

That's not how it should go

Nothing is impossible for God

Looking for something better

Street life – a matter of survival

Things are looking up

Sharing God's heart for
the poor

When hope is lost

The start of something new

When I grow up, I would like to be…

Angela and Maria,
Guatemala, July 2003

Reaching out to boys
just like me

Bringing light in the darkness

Treasure in the rubbish

Free to play – valuing every smile

Love conquers all

gentleness. He earned their respect and their love. His maturity considering his background was commendable. It would sometimes have been appropriate to describe him as the mother hen with all her chicks!

Giovani is now back with his family and looking to the future. It is so encouraging to see how he has matured, developed and progressed, and maintained those wonderful qualities of kindness and graciousness. Here is his story, told in his own words.

My Story – Giovani

In 1997, when I was 8 years old, I used to work selling mirrors. However, I had a bad habit. I used to play on arcade games and I would spend all the money I earned from the mirrors on these games. When I had spent all my money, my mum used to hit me. When I was this age another bad thing happened; my brother sexually abused me. Because of these things and because of other family problems, I made the decision to leave my home and to choose street life.

I went to Zone 6 of Guatemala City. I stayed at a petrol station asking people for money from 7pm at night until 5am in the morning. After that I used to go to the town of Antigua to play on the arcade machines. It was always like this until I got to know a group of young people on the street from a gang called 18. They told me that a ministry had come and they were helping people to leave the streets. The gang spoke to the people from the ministry and they agreed to take me on and I was able to join a children's home supported by Toybox in 1998.

I behaved well and so in 2000 God gave me the privilege of going to the UK. I had a great experience in England. I was able to share my story with many people; I never thought that would happen. I visited London, Scotland and many other places and I returned to Guatemala very happy. I carried on in the home and with God.

In 2001, I went again to England for fifteen days and met new people and made new friends. I was able to go to Northern and Southern Ireland. When I came back, I gave thanks to God for the privilege that he gave me to know such a beautiful country. I carried on in the home and with studying and with my walk with God.

In 2003, I left the home supported by Toybox and began the process of independent living. I was pleased to be able to return to my family – especially to my mum. At church, I have the privilege of serving God by being the sound engineer. I am also able to work selling dishes. In addition, I study on Saturdays and, thanks to God, I passed the 5th grade of accounting. I just have one more year to do and I will graduate as an accountant. I will be able to find a good job and I will be able to help my mum so that she can stop working.

I ask for your help in prayer, that God gives me strength. God bless you and thanks for everything.

5

Someone to Notice Me: A faint glimmer of hope in the darkness

"When Jesus Christ asked the little children to come to him, he didn't say only the rich children, or white children, or children with two-parent families, or children who didn't have a mental or physical handicap. He said, 'Let all children come unto me'."

Marian Wright Edelman

Prior to my first placement in Latin America, I had never really thought through the difficulties that children may face in choosing to leave the streets. I had, very naively, assumed that you could simply pick children up from the streets in a minibus, take them to a home and they would live happily ever after. I realised that there may be some problems along the way but nothing on the scale of what the reality is.

From the streets to a home

In general, the younger a child is, the easier it is to help them and the more quickly they seem to adapt to life off the streets. In general, it is also fair to say that the sooner you get to a child, the easier it is to help them – this is something we refer to as early encounters. If you can find a child within the first few days, or even hours, of them arriving on the streets, you are more likely to be able to help them to successfully participate in a programme. The longer the child lives on the streets, the more accustomed they become to this style of life. They build friendship groups or become part of a gang which often acts as a surrogate family for the child. They often become addicted to solvents or other types of drug and are less able to think rationally about the choices on offer. They are also susceptible to being forced into dangerous and exploitative types of work which can be hard to escape from.

Many organisations have developed processes which help those children who can't be reunited with their families to make the change from life on the streets to life in a home. Stage one is obviously where the street team come in. Their job is to visit the children and young people on the streets and to earn their trust. Many of the children are distrustful of adults, which is not really surprising when you consider that for many kids, the majority of the adults they have met have had a negative impact on their lives. Their parents may have abused them or thrown them out of home. Shopkeepers may have shouted at them for sleeping in their shop doorway. The police or security forces may have hurt them or their friends and passers-by may have been rude to them. When some other adults come along and say they want to help, it would be quite understandable for these children to question why.

Earning the trust of the children requires commitment on the part of the team. If you say you will turn up at 3pm the next day with a football then it is really important that you do so. It is also important that the children see that you are consistent with them. They prefer to have boundaries and to have the security of knowing how the workers will react to them in various circumstances.

A sticky plaster for the heart?

From my time working on the streets, I quickly learnt that the one thing that the children really want more than anything is attention. They want someone to notice them. This was never more evident than when the first aid kit came out! Giving first aid is an important way to help the children. You can imagine that if you live by the side of the city rubbish dump and you get a cut on your leg, it could very easily get infected. First aid treatment is also a really practical way of demonstrating to the children that we care about them and they are important. On many occasions there were children there who needed our care but there were also lots of other children who liked to pretend that they did. The first aid kit would appear, and within minutes, a queue of children would form, some with genuine reasons, others with slightly less obvious ones. As each child would be treated in turn, it was interesting to hear what they said.

I recall a young girl saying "I have a scar on my hand. It is from an accident I had a few years ago. It has been fine for years and now suddenly it's started to hurt again. I think I need a plaster on it." It was obvious to all of us that there was nothing wrong with her hand. All she wanted was a little bit of one-on-one attention for a while. She wanted someone to care, someone to be interested in her and someone to listen to her hurts and concerns.

There were occasions when the injuries were too serious and we needed to take the children to a local hospital for treatment. Sometimes we needed to pay for this but it was all part of the care on offer. There were times when the children would take us to see their friends who were injured, secure in the fact that we would take the necessary action to ensure that if at all possible we could provide the medical care they needed.

The organisation gives help and advice to those people who need it and they are good people who help us to move forward with our lives.

Simeon, aged 15 years

Knife and fork training – pizza style!

Those children who are unable to live with their families but who want to leave the streets and to move into some type of alternative care, often require a lot of help and support to do so. In these situations, the next step in the journey is to invite the child to attend some kind of day centre. It was through working in such a centre that I really learnt more of the struggles these children go through and the issues they have to deal with. It was there that I met a young boy called Luis, aged about 8 years.

Luis lived by the side of a rubbish dump, although he was a fairly transient lad and could be found in various other locations from time to time. He was very independent and very tough. Nothing appeared to bother him. He was small in height and appeared underweight but he was surviving in an adult world. He was making it on his own and from the outside he seemed to have everything under control. However, once in the day centre, the obvious gaps in his learning began to become apparent.

Luis had never been to school and didn't even know how to write his own name. Not only that, the concept of using a knife and fork appeared completely alien to him. Despite attempts from the staff to get him to try to use them he continued to resist. In the end it was decided that the best thing to do would be to set him a challenge. Luis was told that if he could learn to use his knife and fork and show us how well he could use them then we would take him, and the other eight boys who were attending the centre, out for a pizza at a local restaurant. As pizza was Luis' favourite food he was very keen to rise to the challenge and remarkably, within a few days, he had pretty much mastered the art of eating politely. And so it was that the day came for us all to go out to eat. For many of these kids it was the first time they had been to a restaurant. Preparing to go was quite a time-consuming event. Each of the boys wanted to have a shower at the centre and they changed into some clean clothes. As a group they were a lot quieter than they usually were – a mixture of excitement and nerves filled the air. I was so proud of them that day. They were so well behaved and a pleasure to be with. Luis was very pleased with himself and the other boys were obviously overjoyed that his success had resulted in them enjoying a meal out.

The next day came and the boys were back at the day

centre. The morning activities passed and it was time for lunch. Today it was to be black beans, rice and tortillas. Not quite the same as the previous day's pizza, but nonetheless a fairly typical dish and one that the boys liked to eat. Following the success of the previous day I expected lunch to be no problem at all but young Luis had other ideas. Now that he had won the pizza challenge he decided to revert to his old eating styles and the knife and fork were abandoned once again. Still, at least he now knew how to use them!

I see a future where I am a good person, helping other people in the way you are helping me.

Carol, aged 12 years

Moving on step by step

It is lovely to see the changes in the children as they spend more and more time off the streets and as they are cared for and encouraged to learn new things.

However, it's not an easy journey and often there needs to be another step between the streets and the homes. This can be a halfway house or some kind of hostel, which allows the children to get used to sleeping inside, living with others, obeying rules and getting used to routine.

This is probably the hardest part of the process. Although choosing to leave the streets brings many positive things it also has its difficulties and challenges. The children may be leaving behind their gang or their surrogate street family. They may also be leaving behind their drugs to which the levels of addiction can be very strong. In addition to this, by choosing to participate in a centre or hostel, they are by default choosing to sacrifice some of the freedoms they have when on the streets.

> **Now I don't sleep in the street, I have a bed and a place to sleep.**
>
> *Max, aged 17 years*

> **God has taken me from the streets and the teachers help me.**
>
> *Alfonso, aged 17 years*

No favourite children!

Before I went out to Latin America for the first time, someone told me that it was really important not to have favourite children. I tried very hard to stick to that. But, if you pushed me really hard and asked me about those kids that had made the biggest impression on me, then a young lad called Marcos would come pretty high on my list. I lived with Marcos in his home for a couple of weeks in the autumn of 1999. Home for Marcos at that point was a special home for street mums and their children. He was there with his mum and his younger brother and sister. He was a quiet, thoughtful boy, who would generally keep himself to himself. Often appearing troubled, it was clear that things had been, and continued to be, very difficult for this young lad. However, despite that, Marcos was also just an ordinary boy. He had a lovely smile and when encouraged he could do well both academically and in the sporting arena.

Before arriving at the home, time had been given to planning a list of activities that we could run with the children. As it was the school holidays we expected the children to need entertaining all day every day – we knew we needed to be prepared! However, despite all the preparation we did, there was one very basic activity that captured the imagination of Marcos – colouring in. He just loved it and never seemed to get bored, so long as you would give time to him and admire each picture that he produced. I recall many a morning where my alarm clock was in fact Marcos, banging on my bedroom door shouting "Vamos a Pintar!" which is Spanish for 'Let's do some colouring!' I was never quite sure where he got his energy from but it was lovely to see him happy and excited about the day ahead.

Unfortunately, things didn't work out for Marcos in the way that we hoped they would. The aim was to support Marcos, his mum and her other two children (Cristina and Gabriel) through this difficult time and eventually to assist them to move into their own flat and to live independently from the charity. In the end this just wasn't possible. In this report from two of the staff members who worked with Marcos and his family, we get to see just why things didn't turn out the way that we had hoped. Along with their son Alex, this dedicated couple had tried to do all they could to help this family move on but the story didn't end in the way they had either hoped or anticipated.

Staff member report

Love at first sight? With an age gap of 11 years? But that was how it was for our son Alex and baby Cristina back in 2000. To our 11-year-old son, Cristina was a cute little baby who was dreadfully neglected by her mother, often left alone in their bedroom

crying with pain brought about by dirty nappies left unchanged for hours. Alex became very adept at changing nappies and cuddling the little girl who was to be totally abandoned by her mother a year or two later.

For Cristina's part, Alex was the first person who had ever taken a real interest in her and she adored being around him. A few months after their first encounter, when she was beginning to make intelligible sounds, she would bounce up and down in her high chair when Alex entered the room shouting out "Da da, da da". This should not be misconstrued! Her young man would often let his own food go cold as he fed her while her mother was too busy eating or hitting Cristina's two brothers.

One incident stands out among many. Gabriel, aged 2, dropped some food on the floor. His mother sent Marcos, Gabriel's older brother, to the kitchen to get a wooden spatula. When he returned, his mother hit Gabriel very hard, publicly, with it for his huge "sin" of dropping food. This is the same woman who made Gabriel sit for hours in his high chair. When we asked her to let him play with the other little ones, she said that he couldn't because he always hit them. Wonder why!

Marcos fared no better. He would be beaten for the smallest of things. I remember finding him once behind one of the buildings at the home, whimpering like a small wounded animal. I sat there, cuddling him for ten minutes while he continued to whimper. I eventually led him to our little house where we lived on site and, after a few chocolate biscuits and many more hugs, he whispered to me that he had got some dirt on his one and only coat and that his mother had beaten him.

Anna, the mother, went off one day and never came back. Her three young children are now in homes, Marcos and Gabriel together in a home for boys and Cristina in a girls' home. It is a joy to see the three of them thriving, happily playing with friends and doing well at school. It is not good for children to be separated from their parents but, hey, I guess there are exceptions!

Seven years later, it still hasn't been possible to reunite Marcos, Gabriel or Cristina with their family but they are continuing to progress and be supported. It has been a joy for me to see them grow up as I have made my regular visits to their homes over the last seven years. My pictures of their smiling faces and my memories of our times spent together are ones I deeply cherish. Here's what they had to say recently.

Gabriel, aged 9 – Food, bikes and more food!

I like playing hide and seek, watching TV, participating in discipleship and learning about Jesus. I like it when I play on the bike. I also like the food that they give me and I like the kitchen because that is where they prepare the food. In the future I would like to be a fireman. I like school. This year I learnt to read and write. Also I learnt to ride a bike. I find it hard being without my mum and when the other children fight with me. My best memories in life are of riding a bike, getting presents at Christmas, having fruit punch and tamales (a type of food). In my country, I like the place called

Panajachel and I like the little boats. If I could change one thing in the world it would be not to have fighting. I once went on holiday to my aunt's house. I played on the bike in my uncle's house and I played with my cousins. Once I had an accident with the bike. I hurt my tongue and I had to have stitches.

Cristina, aged 5 – Being my own hairdresser!

I like playing with dolls and playing in the swimming pool. I like my house, the TV and the music. In the future I would like to be a doctor to cure people. Since I was little I have lived here and felt happy. I get sad when it's not my turn for visits because my aunt can't come to visit. The best memory of my life was when we celebrated my birthday. I like sweets and cake a lot! I would like to tell people that in my country we worship and pray to God with all of our heart. My country is very beautiful because it has flowers, mountains and volcanoes. If I could change one thing in the world I would change all the bad things for good things! I have been to warm swimming pools on holiday. I like playing in the pools with Jasmin and Diana. Once a funny thing happened to me. I took scissors secretly and ran behind the house. I grabbed the front bit of my hair and cut it to the top and I looked very funny. Thank God it's grown back now!

Marcos, aged 12 – Life in my new home

Now I'm a helpful boy with what they ask me to do. One of the nicest things was when we went to the cinema for the first time in my life. Another

experience was the trip to Xocomil, a huge water park, which I liked a lot and I was very happy. I like learning Bible verses and learning about God. I hope to be with my family again some day.

Ideally, children like Marcos would be living with their parents but this is not always possible. Although it is sad when this can't happen, at least children like Marcos now have some kind of hope of a better future. Where children are unable to be with their own parents, for whatever reason, it is down to staff in local organisations to look for alternative solutions. Sometimes it is possible to place children with members of their extended family or with foster families. Where none of these options are available, then small, family-style children's homes, run by local people, are the best that can be offered. However, this type of security comes with a price tag. Offering long-term committed care is expensive and organisations like Toybox can only fund it through the committed support of regular donors. The odds can be stacked against the children in many ways but for those who really want to make it, change can be a real possibility. The glimmer of hope in the darkness is there for the taking.

6

Free to Play:
A chance to be children

"Children are the world's most valuable resource and
its best hope for the future."

John F. Kennedy

As soon as the children realised that visitors were
arriving they ran towards the gate, faces smiling, eyes
expectant and voices full of excitement. The visitors were
Clare, Mark and me. We had come to the home Malquias
to meet the children and mums who lived there, children
we would be working with during our time in Guatemala.
We had hardly had time to leave the minibus before the
younger children were jumping into our arms. The boys
were intrigued by Mark's blond hair, something they
don't often see in Guatemala, and they took great delight
in chasing him around the grounds. Rachel, our guide,
soon settled them down, seating them around tables in
the living room. It was just like visiting a huge family.
These children knew that visitors meant lots of attention
and lots of playmates! It struck me what a transition in
trust they had made. On the streets, it can take weeks to
gain the trust of a child who has been living rough.

By this time the mums had also made their way up to see us, slightly more cautious but equally welcoming in their approach. We spent around an hour cutting, sticking and gluing pieces of coloured paper together in a specially designed craft activity which the children loved.

This was followed by hours of play in the extensive grounds of the home. I've never had so much fun playing with children as I did that day! The resources we had were quite basic but the children didn't mind at all and were content to devise games out of the things we had. The younger children, such as Joshua and Sonia, were keen to spend as much time as possible on the swings, which were situated in the middle of the garden. Although quite able to swing themselves, they loved to have someone to push them just that little bit higher and would scream with delight each time it happened. Alejandro was a little bit older and he loved to play ball sports; football and tennis were his favourites. Although he seemed to find it hard to mix with the others, once engaged in an activity his determination was evident. He certainly displayed a natural talent for sport.

Although the children were all individuals with their own favourite activities, there was one thing that they all wanted to join in with. In the process of playing with the children, Mark picked one of them up and spun them around a couple of times. Suddenly all the children wanted a go and Clare and I were also asked to help out. Some wanted to be spun around by their hands, others by one foot and one hand, each trying to see if they could sing a song while being spun around! Their joy and excitement was contagious and none of us wanted the day to end.

The children were so proud of their home, keen to show us around and content to spend their time playing simple games and just enjoying being children.

We celebrate birthdays with photos, cake and more.

The Cruz family (mum and three kids) who used to live on the streets of Guatemala

The huge contrast between the children on the streets and those now living within the security and love of a home is incredible. It is something which struck me so strongly that first day I visited and never ceases to amaze me every time I go back. Not that the transition to a home is easy, as the earlier chapters of this book have shown, but for those who do make it and who adapt to a new kind of lifestyle there lies the freedom to play, the freedom to be children and the opportunity to make choices about the way they want their life to be.

Introducing Diana

I first met Diana the day she left the streets and began the process of moving into a home. She was about 4 or 5 years old. I entered the day-centre building and saw her standing in the yard. She didn't look well and appeared either unwilling or unable to speak. As I learnt a little more about her background I began to understand why.

Prior to this day, Diana could frequently be seen wandering the streets dressed in a vest and underwear with no shoes on, looking dirty and with scars on her face. She had hardly any hair on her head, just patches.

It had either been pulled out or it had fallen out due to malnutrition. She often appeared scared of everyone around her and didn't talk, but instead screamed words which no one could make out. Her mum was usually nowhere to be seen. Diana was often found alone in the middle of the red-light district, surrounded by drunks, drug addicts and prostitutes, completely vulnerable and scared.

She was skinny. She had probably never had a decent meal in her life, living instead on food she had begged for or scraps that her mum had given to her. Her mum made a living by selling her body and wasn't able to look after Diana very well. Although she already had two older children who had moved into charity homes, Diana and her little brother were still on the streets, struggling to survive.

When one of the teams started working in this red-light district they found a number of children who were in need, Diana being the most desperate. She was wary of the team at first, taking time to check them out. They took it slowly, visiting her for a little while longer each time until one day, when they finally made a breakthrough. Diana came closer and closer to one of the team members until she was actually sitting on her lap. She rested her head against her chest and played with a lollipop the team had given to her. She stayed there for what seemed like a very long time and when it was time for the team to leave she didn't want to let go. They wondered if that was the first time she'd ever been hugged.

After speaking to the social worker and psychologist and emphasising the urgency of the situation, everyone agreed to speed the process along so that Diana could move into a safe environment. Her mother agreed it would be best for her to leave the streets as long as she could visit her.

As Diana had such special needs and displayed significant behavioural problems, the decision was made for her to live with one of the staff members for a short time before moving on to life in a home. Although this was difficult for her she slowly began to settle down.

Staff member report

The day that Diana walked though my door into my house she was crying and scared. She was wearing only her shorts and t-shirt and she wanted her mum, who was still on the street with her little brother.

She would not change her clothes because that was the only thing that she felt safe with. She would go to bed with her shoes and coat on, as she thought that she would be ready when her mum came. She couldn't understand that her mum was never going to come.

Diana found it very hard to listen to anyone who was trying to help her. She wouldn't eat and just kept saying that her food and new clothes were for her little brother who was still on the streets. I finally got her to eat when I made a plate of food for her and another one for her brother. I told her that my boss would come when she had gone to sleep and take the plate to her brother. This seemed to work very well!

Diana went through a very hard time but has come out with flying colours. As soon as she moved into one of the homes she was a very different little girl, who was very happy. She has put on weight and her hair has grown enough so that she can have it up in pigtails. She is very happy, living with her big sister, running around laughing, dancing, singing, playing and having a lot of fun. She is amazing, precious and now has a hope for the future.

One year on from my first encounter with Diana, I asked her about her life now. Here's what she had to say.

The things I like doing – Diana, aged 5 years

My favourite thing is dolls. I like playing with Jasmin and I like my house. In the future I want to be a teacher. I used to live with my mum, Lilian. I washed dishes, did cleaning and looked after Alex (my little brother). I felt sad because my mum Lilian used to kick me really hard. My best memories in life are of playing with Alex. I liked it when we went to Pollo Campero (fast food chicken restaurant) - I like the games there. I felt really happy. A funny thing happened here. I was playing with Jasmin, I bit a piece off her big toenail and then I asked for forgiveness!

As mentioned before, it often seems that the younger the child is when they arrive in a home, the easier it is for them to make the transition to a new way of life. However, the transformation certainly isn't reserved for the young, as the testimonies of young adults like Andres show. There are some amazingly resilient and resourceful young people on the streets of Latin America and, given the right support and opportunities, they will often choose to fight for a better way of life and for the chance to fulfil their potential.

From a young puppy to a fine dog!

Andres and his older brother, Giovani, grew up in the streets with their mother, who was unable to care for them properly. Both boys would have to steal to get food and grew very tired of living on the streets. Their mother asked a local organisation for help and both boys were offered a place in a boys' home in August 1997, when Andres was 9 years of age. It has been a real privilege to watch Andres grow up since that time. He has the most amazing smile and a lovely personality. He has got into his fair share of trouble over the years and can be more than a little bit cheeky, but it is great that he has been able to be a normal child and teenager. As this next report shows, he is growing up into a fine young man.

Andres – A teacher's report

Andres always reminded me of a great big puppy, full of energy and getting into trouble, then looking at you with big soulful eyes that say "Sorry, I didn't really mean it". He bounced in and out of our lives for a year or two, meeting up at the various events we had for all the homes together.

We finally came face to face in Music and English classes as I took on my part-time role as teacher in the ministry-run school. Oh dear! Classes were never dull! We continually clashed over invisible homework and incessant tooting of his recorder in all the inappropriate places. He is, in fact, quite a musician but not in the formal sense of the word.

The puppy is beginning to grow into a fine dog and spends less time straining at the lead. I had not seen him for quite some time when we turned up at one of the homes, Shalom, for a birthday party. Andres was there with some other lads from the other homes. Along with some of the Shalom girls, they were trying to put together a formal dance to perform at a wedding. It centred around some waltz-like movements in couples – with the problem being that none of them could waltz!

Suddenly ex-teacher finds herself leading ex-pupil around the floor, pushing his feet this way and that to a "one, two, three" beat, whilst the others look on and take note. Pupil is now several inches taller than teacher and is at long last finding his own two feet, not only in the waltz but in that big confusing world that he is going to have to go out into someday without adults to lead him. I'm confident he's going to do just great.

We recently chatted to Andres about his life, what he wants to do in the future and what he thinks of his country. This is what he had to say...

Let me tell you about my life – Andres, aged 17 years

I've been living in the home Emmanuel. I've studied, I've gone to church and I've shared with many people. They took me off the street and they gave me housing, clothes and a new and different life. I've gone through difficult moments but I've overcome them and I've been happy with my housemates. My favourite thing is playing football. In the future I would like to be an architect. I find it hard when

someone doesn't like me or get on with me. If I could change one thing in the world I would change the disobedience that there is. My best memory is when we all went out one day to Rio Dulce and to San Felipe Castle. My country is a very beautiful place. It has touristy places which everyone would like to visit. I enjoyed my holiday to Rio Dulce and I like being together like a family.

Staying in the children's homes is a real privilege and each one has its own highlights. Staying with the younger children was a mixture of exhausting, thrilling and challenging. These children have so much energy and don't like to see you sitting around for more than a couple of minutes! Life in the older children's homes is altogether a different experience, as you might expect. The mornings were more laid back with everyone taking the opportunity to get as much sleep as possible. School, homework and vocational training were much more part of the routine but the sense of family and hope for the future was still very much part of life.

Every night we pray to God and we give thanks to God for all he has given.

Maria, aged 13 years

Fernando – A family to call his own

In 2001, a number of people in the UK were given the opportunity to meet two of the boys from Guatemala when Giovani and Fernando came on a trip to the UK. The boys travelled to London with the director of the organisation that was caring for them. They joined staff from Toybox in a UK tour, which saw them visiting schools and churches in a variety of locations. The tour event was a combination of talks from staff, video footage, drama, songs and photos. During the event, both Giovani and Fernando were also interviewed and given the chance to tell their own story from their own perspective. The boys seemed to really enjoy the opportunity that this trip gave them as they visited London, learnt to ice-skate and had their first ever go on a rollercoaster. Their trip to the UK and the simple and honest way in which they told their story certainly had an impact on those who heard it. We were all touched by the account of a lady from Kirkheaton who met Fernando and then wrote to us at the office to tell us about her encounter with him – a child whom she had now held in her arms.

Children I had held in my arms

I wanted to tell you of something I saw when Fernando and the rest of the team came to Kirkheaton. While you were on stage, the boys had come over to where I was standing, by the stall. Fernando stood and stared for nearly ten minutes watching a mother and her son. He was totally oblivious to the fact that I was watching him look at Joyce and Angus. Angus is 7 and he was sitting on his mum's knee. He was stroking her face and quietly whispering to her. His mum was cuddling him, kissing his face and stroking his hair. Neither knew that they were being watched. Slowly and quietly, Fernando moved closer and closer until he stood right by them. Just so that he could be part of what he saw, he began to give Angus sweets, one at a time. Fernando stayed there until he was called on stage.

When the interview was over he came off stage and walked back up to Joyce and Angus, again standing just slightly behind them. I think at this point he must have become aware of the fact that I was watching him, as he turned to look at me and smiled. As I held out my hands to him he ran straight into them and hugged and hugged me. When I lifted up his young face to kiss him on the forehead his face was wet with tears.

It was only when I read the October issue of the newsletter and read of the fact that he had suffered years of abuse by his mum that the full force of why he'd stood for so long, looking so longingly at Joyce and Angus, hit home to me. Then from somewhere deep inside of me came the tears. I sobbed and sobbed as I recalled in my mind the look on his face and the longing in his eyes. My heart cut so deep – these were no longer children thousands of miles away, but were children I had held in my arms.

After two weeks in England it was time for the boys to head back home to Guatemala. Although they had both enjoyed their visit, they were clearly ready to get back to some warmer weather, people who spoke Spanish and some decent Guatemalan cooking! The staff member who brought them had arranged to stay on in the UK for a while so I agreed to accompany Giovani and Fernando on their return flight to Guatemala.

We arrived at Heathrow airport early in the morning and checked in ready to board our flight. Anyone who has made a journey such as this will know that it makes for a very long day. The first flight took us from London to Miami, where we waited for a while before catching the second flight down to Guatemala City. Fernando was normally a happy and easy-going young lad, but by the time we got to Guatemala he was certainly not his normal cheerful self. I think this could be attributed to the fact that he was hungry; he hadn't particularly liked the aeroplane food. He was also tired, which was probably a combination of a hectic two weeks followed by two long flights and a seven-hour time difference. Having got off the plane, we collected our suitcases and began walking slowly and quietly through the airport building. Guatemala airport has a balcony around the edge of it, which acts as a kind of viewing gallery. As we were walking towards the exit, we suddenly heard shouts from above. There on the balcony were children from Fernando's home along with some of the staff. Some were holding banners, others shouted and all were smiling and waving to us. As Fernando saw them his face broke into a smile.

He turned towards me and said, "Look, Ange, it's my family! They've come to pick me up from the airport".

He forgot his tiredness and hunger and was immediately full of joy again. He was quickly through the airport doors and there were hugs all round and lots of people to welcome him home. No longer left to survive on his own, Fernando now had security, love and a place to belong.

I want to form my own family! – Fernando, aged 18 years

Now I live in Emmanuel home and since I was little I have always lived here. I started studying to be a teacher this year, but unfortunately it wasn't my vocation and I stopped halfway through the year. Now I will start to study a higher secondary school course in hotel business and tourism. I am hoping it will go well. I think this stage in my life is hard because with youth comes many tests and one has to decide whether to follow the good or the bad that friends offer.

I like to cook, play basketball and watch TV. Of course, there are many things I find difficult; for example, I find maths and physics hard. I like to watch TV and read all types of books. In the future I want to work in what I graduate in and get involved more in the things of God. Most importantly, I want to form my own family.

My best memory that I have is to have gone to England, especially to get to know a little about the English culture, to know London and other special places in England and to get to know other people.

Guatemala is a country characterised by mountains. The climate is varied – not too cold nor too hot. It also has lovely touristy places like the ruins of Tikal in Peten and the San Felipe Castle in Rio Dulce. They also say that it's a country blessed by God and there are many Christian churches. My best holiday was five years ago when we went to Rio Dulce and San Felipe Castle. It was very beautiful. We enjoyed it. We played, ate and swam, just like a family.

Fernando's home, Emmanuel, certainly has a family atmosphere, as I discovered when I stayed there for a couple of weeks with another volunteer. One evening in particular stands out in my mind. It was the night that the houseparents decided they needed a night off and that it would be fine for us to look after the ten boys on our own! We were slightly apprehensive as the parents left, but they encouraged us that it would be fine – "Just let them watch TV until around 8pm and then send them all to bed," they said as they waved goodbye to us all. So, there we were all watching TV together when suddenly, in an advert break at around 7pm, Hector, who at 14 was the oldest of the boys, got up and turned off the TV. Feeling slightly pessimistic at this point I figured that they were about to do something they shouldn't, but I needn't have worried at all. Hector turned to the boys and said, "Right boys, we haven't prayed today or said thank you to God for all we have and normally we would do that with Mum and Dad before bed, but they're not here so I think we should do it anyway, Amen?" – all the boys replied, "Amen!"

Within about 30 seconds, all the boys had jumped up, formed a circle by the TV and were beckoning us to come and join them. Hector read a few verses from the Bible and led the boys in a couple of children's songs with actions. Then they began to pray and the only thing they said when they prayed that night was "Thank you". Thank you, God for this house, for food to eat and clothes to wear. Thank you for football, TV, for people in England who send money to pay for our school fees. And so it went on. Towards the end of the prayer time the focus changed towards the future as some of the boys began to pray, "Thank you God that in the future I can be... a footballer, a doctor, someone who helps the street children". Once they had all had chance to pray, Hector turned the TV back on and the boys continued to watch their programmes until 8pm, when they went to bed as planned.

Once they had gone to bed and the house was quiet again I had time to sit and think about what had happened that evening. It was such a privilege to see boys who had once lived on the streets now living in a home together as a family, now happy and now so grateful for all that they have. Their gratitude to God was such a challenge to me. I knew that back in England I had so much more than these boys would probably ever have but I also knew that I often took it for granted. These boys not only valued the new life they had now, but they also had dreams and visions for the future; they knew that life could be different.

For Fernando, Diana, Andres, the Emmanuel boys and the many other children in the homes, adapting to a new lifestyle has been hard and there continue to be challenges for all of them. However, these stories show that change really is possible. No longer surviving on the streets with little hope of change, these children and young people are taking brave new steps and are striving for something better.

Christmas in my home

Hello! Dear friends, I am called Fernando. I want to thank you for the support that you bring to all here

in Guatemala. Now, I want to tell you a little about what happened at Christmas here in the home Emmanuel. During the day, the Christmas meal was prepared. In the evening we went to church and returned about 10pm. We watched TV and waited for midnight when we ate the Christmas meal and gave Christmas hugs.

Everything was good. God bless you. Sincerely, Fernando.

7

Reality Hits:
A matter of life and death

"In the little world in which children have their
existence, whosoever brings them up, there is nothing
so finely perceived and so finely felt as injustice."

Charles Dickens

The toothpaste boy

Daniel was in the process of trying to leave the streets.
When I first met him it was during a day with the street
team. We went to visit his 'home'; a self-constructed
shelter where he and numerous other young people were
camping out. To be fair to them, they had worked really
hard on making it seem like a home. The sides were
made out of corrugated iron, plastic, cardboard and bits
of metal. Over the top was a large piece of black plastic
sheeting. Inside the 'den', the place was pretty messy but
they had managed to find an old, very worn-looking sofa
and an even older-looking and very dirty mattress, which
they all shared between them. Pinned up on the 'walls'
were some of the pictures and craft items that they had

made during activities with the street team. The shelter didn't look too sturdy and it certainly wasn't completely waterproof, but for these kids it was a home. Located in one of the most dangerous zones of Guatemala City, their aim was to stick together and to be some kind of family for each other.

This group was usually pretty keen to be involved in the activities on offer but showed little desire for change. Many had been on the streets for years. Levels of addiction to solvents and other types of drug were high and they were prepared to do almost anything to get the drugs and the money they needed. Although Daniel had been on the streets with them for some time, he was different. He did want to leave the streets; he was interested in what was on offer. And so it was that he began to attend the day centre.

Daniel was pretty anxious as he started at the day centre. He had been worried that his 'family' back at the 'den' would feel like he was rejecting them but they seemed surprisingly supportive and were happy to let him come along. He must have been about 14 or 15 years of age and was one of the oldest attending the day centre at that time. During the first week in the centre, part of the programme involved lessons on basic things such as cleaning your teeth. I'll never forget Daniel taking part in this!

Prior to the lesson, I had been asked to prepare a poster showing how you should clean your teeth and why it is important to do so. My art skills are less than brilliant but somehow they managed to make use of it! The staff member proceeded to explain how to use the brush properly to get at all the teeth and he handed out a brand new toothbrush and a large tube of toothpaste to each of the children. Most of the kids didn't seem too excited about their new possessions but Daniel was incredibly enthusiastic. He immediately got up and went to the outside sink to begin cleaning his teeth.

A couple of minutes later, I went outside to do some jobs for the team and I saw Daniel at the sink. I watched with amusement as I saw Daniel squirting the toothpaste straight out of the tube and into his mouth and then brushing his teeth in a repetitive way. Unfortunately, his aim with the toothpaste was not always accurate and paste was also landing on his clothes and in the sink. Daniel was the kind of boy who looked unbelievably innocent and sweet, but could be incredibly cheeky and just a little bit naughty! I went over to him and showed him how to put the toothpaste on his brush. He seemed pleased to learn an additional part of the process and then continued to brush. I went away to do some jobs and came back what must have been about five or six minutes later. Daniel was still brushing his teeth. I watched him as he put a small amount of paste on his brush and brushed his teeth. He then put some more paste on his brush, brushed his teeth, and so on. I decided to go over to have a chat with him and quickly established that Daniel thought you were meant to use the whole tube of toothpaste, every time you brushed your teeth! Daniel was about 15 and he had never brushed his teeth before. Not only that, he didn't even know what to do. In so many ways he was so very grown up but in others he was just like a toddler.

Daniel successfully completed the programme in the day centre and moved into a small family-style home. Over the next few years I watched as Daniel changed and grew up. He began to emerge into a fine young man who cared deeply for the younger boys around him. He loved to play football and he wanted to be a mechanic when he grew up.

Then one year, when I returned, Daniel was no longer there. He had decided to leave the home. No one really understood why and neither did Daniel; he just left. That year I met Daniel when I was out on the streets with the street team. He remembered me from the previous years and we had a bit of a chat. He told me that he realised he wasn't doing well. He was back on drugs and back with his old friends. He told me he didn't know why and he knew it wasn't good, but it was his choice.

Although we would love to be able to tell you that every story has a happy ending, this just isn't the case. Daniel hasn't returned to a centre or home and, as far as I know, continues to live on the streets. Not every child that has contact with an organisation will successfully manage to build a new life off the streets. Not every child who shows the desire to work for a better life will achieve what they want to achieve. At times like this it is easy to question why. Should things have been done differently; was there something missing from the support that Daniel had? It is good for organisations to ask these kinds of questions; it is part of learning and refining the work that is done. However, sometimes there is no obvious answer. We can never force the children to make use of the services on offer. Sometimes they may choose things that we may not think are the best for them. However, they have to be free to make that choice. The reality is that work with street children will have its difficulties and disappointments. That's just the way things are and that's part of the challenge of the work.

In memory of Ernesto

Another lad who was around at the same time as Daniel was a boy called Ernesto. My overriding memory is of Ernesto playing on a brightly coloured bouncing duck at a local park. Despite the fact that he was well into his teenage years, he was a real child at heart and he just loved to play and to be the entertainer.

Ernesto's story

I was born on 6 January 1985 in the Republic of Honduras in Central America. I was the youngest of three brothers. My biological father separated from my mother and she decided to get together with another partner. My stepfather mistreated me and for this reason I decided to go to the streets. An organisation in Honduras looked after me when I was young, but I often escaped from there. I would usually go back though because if I didn't, my mum would find me, and I didn't want to live in my home so it was better to be with an organisation.

In 1994, when I was 9 years old, I made the decision to leave for Guatemala. Once in Guatemala, I also had to live on the streets, although various homes and charities did give me attention. These were hard and difficult times for me.

On 28 January in 2000, a street team started spending time with me and I started to go to a day centre. From there I moved into a hostel and then, on 11 September that same year, I was able to move into a home called Maranatha. I lived there and shared many happy and sad times with the other boys.

What I liked most was to eat Pollo Campero (fast-food chicken) and to play football. While I lived in the home, I also went to church. What I didn't like to do was to study! I found it so very difficult to concentrate and I preferred to go to work. I started working in a garage and I would spray-paint cars during the day. It was there that I learnt this trade well.

When I got older, I moved into the process of Social Reintegration. I was living near to a town called Chimaltenango. I carried on working in the spray-painting garage until the owner told me that I couldn't carry on working there.

During my time in Social Reintegration, I had many happy moments of sharing with the ladies and the young men who were also taking part in this process. One happy moment was at Easter. We went to a water park, we swam and we played. We also broke piñatas to celebrate the birthdays of everyone taking part in the Social Reintegration process. We had presents and we all ate together – it was really happy. A funny moment the same day was when the lady in charge asked, "Who knows the way to the centre?" I offered myself as a guide. The funny thing was when we had to cross some streets. There was a teacher driving the van and I didn't tell him early enough when he would need to turn and so he had to keep turning around. We all laughed and they told me that, as a co-pilot, I was just making them get lost!

After my job in the car garage, it was difficult finding another job, but one day I found one and I started working in another spray-painting garage in the capital, Guatemala City. The owner was very pleased with the way I was and with my work because I used the tools and apparatus well. The owner said he identified with me because he was like me when he was young. However, because it was winter time there was hardly any work. So, the owner spoke to my social worker and explained that I couldn't carry on in the workshop for the time being.

From that point onwards, I made a decision that I wouldn't work any more. I had many aspirations; my biggest dream was to have my own spray-painting garage, but sadly I didn't think things through well and I made wrong decisions.

I started frequenting the streets again and I spent time with young people who influenced me negatively. I wanted to have easy money and I got that through robbing people on the streets and on the buses, and by intimidating them with arms. Because of this, I ended up in prison at various times. Life in prison is very hard and you have to adapt if you want to survive. I got hit many times and once it was for defending another boy who was being beaten unjustly. In the prison they called me little Ernie as I was so young to be in a prison which was mainly full of adults.

Ernesto's story had to be written by his social worker based on her experiences of him. I couldn't ask him to write it for himself. The final time that Ernesto came out of prison, someone in a nearby car shot him. He fell to the floor, badly hurt but still alive. He was rushed to hospital and they operated on him immediately. He could have recovered but shortly after the operation he ran away from the hospital and went to the central park of the capital city to see his friends. His body couldn't take it any more and he fell to the ground bleeding. He died very shortly afterwards.

My little star, by Gail Marie, former Toybox gapyear student

I called Ernesto 'my little star', just because he was. We had an instant connection, perhaps because I had worked in his hometown in Honduras. When I first started to talk to Ernesto, for some reason he struggled to remember my name. Instead when he saw me he would shout out 'Honduras' in his deep Honduran accent, and point and wave in my direction.

At times Ernesto, like all the children, would struggle to overcome the haunting of his past, and I would see an angry expression appear on his face as the frustration would begin to show. He wanted to be a man, to be able to take care of himself and move on from needing to be cared for. I remember talking at great length with him about his past and his dealings with the notorious gang '18'. He certainly wasn't proud of his past; Ernesto would always look at the floor when he spoke of his life before Toybox. He didn't like to remember the things he did and I was honoured that he chose to speak of it to me. He had left his hometown to try to move on and become something better. He was proud of his job and of what he was becoming.

Whilst I was working in the home he was living in, he would come home from work covered in the dust of the day and ask me to make his dinner. I couldn't refuse the cheeky smile. Exhausted, he would crash out on the sofa while the younger boys would jump on him. One particular evening he and I tied curtain ties round our heads and battled it out using our made-up karate moves to see who was the strongest; he won of course. But, that very same evening I was to see the gentle side of Ernesto as he decided to paint my nails; he took great care in using the nail brush and almost expertly painting them. It struck me how different he was. I realised what a change had taken place in this young man.

Ernesto loved cowboys; the walk, the talk and especially the look. I think it was the fact that he thought they were real men. He would come swaggering into the kitchen with a cowboy hat on his head, a tea towel tied around his neck and a plastic gun tucked down the front of his trousers. I was to see this look a few times; on one occasion he didn't know I was looking. He was standing in front of the mirror and was practising his swagger; he pulled out the gun and pointed it at the mirror. When he turned and saw me standing there, he fell to the floor in embarrassment and refused to look at me for a while. The sad irony of that memory hits me as I write these words now. Ernesto died trying to be a man.

Ernesto and the football shirt – A lasting legacy

It is difficult for all of us when the children and young people we know make decisions and choices that we feel are not the best for them. The times when this leads to the loss of life are the hardest for everyone to deal with. It's an obvious reality. The streets are a dangerous place to be, characterised by violence, crime, drugs and prostitution. This is no place for anyone, never mind a child. There is nothing that we can do to change what happened to Ernesto but we want to appreciate the time we had with him, the joy and smiles he brought to those around him and the lasting legacy that he leaves behind.

I recently chatted to Hannah, someone else who knew Ernesto. She recalled the time when she was leaving Guatemala and Ernesto gave her a gift. In Guatemala there are two main football teams, the whites and the reds. On arrival in Guatemala, Hannah had decided she liked the reds, much to Ernesto's disgust! The present that Ernesto gave to her was a whites' football shirt. I don't know how much it would have cost, but his wages where he worked at the mechanics were hardly anything. That shirt probably cost him all he had. He could be such a caring lad and he had so much to give to others. Hannah still has that shirt today and the day she found out that he had been killed she wore it. It means so much to Hannah and is all she has to remind her of him – along with the picture in her head of that big beaming smile of his.

That's not how it should go – Chris Rice, member of staff in Guatemala

Ernesto was in love with Marilyn. Marilyn was in love with Ernesto. Ernesto was in the home Maranatha. Marilyn was one of our girls in the home we ran called Shalom. Ernesto and Marilyn kissed, once, in the back of a minibus when Maranatha had given our girls a lift when our minibus broke down. They caused a few ripples, but hey, they were in love!

Ernesto came to my husband and me one day and asked for Marilyn's hand in marriage. We shrugged, laughed and said OK, as one does when a 15-year-old asks for a 14-year-old's hand in marriage. Thereafter, Ernesto called us father-in-law and mother-in-law.

Ernesto ran away from Maranatha, the home we gave him. Marilyn ran away from Shalom, the home we gave her. They didn't run together. Ernesto was shot dead on the streets. Marilyn lives on the streets – we don't know if she even knows that Ernesto is dead. That's how it goes. But that's not how it should go.

No easy explanation

There are no easy answers as to why these things happen; suffering and injustice are complex issues for us all. As I have travelled around the country to various places talking about the work of Toybox, I have heard many people question how God, a God of love, can allow things like this to happen. In answer to that we can look at factors such as human selfishness, the consequences of sin and the hatred humans can have for each other. While these may seem satisfactory at one level, they never quite seem enough to fully satisfy the questioner. At the end of the day, these are still children, often children we may have got to know, and they are children who deserve better. As Chris Rice commented above, "That's how it goes, but that's not how it should go".

Mynor – A future president?

In 1999, I met a baby boy called Mynor and his mum Miriam. Unfortunately, I only met them once, as they decided at that time not to stay in the centre where I met them. However, just a few weeks ago, Mynor came back. He is now in a home, although this time without his mum. From where I stand now, I can look back over those intervening years and see that even in the harder parts of life it is possible to see God at work.

Miriam is the sister of Anna, a lady who was living in a special home for street girls and their children. They both came from an abusive home and she and her sisters were abandoned onto the streets from a young age. Miriam and her baby of 8 months, Mynor, were staying in a hostel. Having lived on the streets for some time, they were now in the process of trying to leave. Miriam didn't know how to care for Mynor. If he cried with hunger, she thought he was whining and that he deserved a smack. The staff lovingly cared for and protected them both. When I met Miriam, she readily handed Mynor over to me or to anybody else who would have him. He was used to being left and he cried a lot. Miriam was looking forward to moving into a home and joining her sister Anna and her two nephews, Marcos and Gabriel. She dreamt of being part of an idyllic family and hoped they could be together and care for one another.

Miriam and Mynor did move into the home and for a time she was happy to be safe. Mynor too started to feel safe and cried less and smiled more. Then the day came. Miriam left the home to return to the streets. In many ways it was the only real home she knew. She took Mynor with her. Anna and her boys stayed, but Anna was worried for her sister. Not long after, Anna also left, abandoning her children to the charity home.

Six years later, a report came through to the Toybox office that a six-year-old orphan boy named Mynor, the cousin of Marcos and Gabriel, had recently moved into their home. On investigation, I found that this was the

Mynor who I met as a baby, only now his mother Miriam was dead. Before she died, she left Mynor with a family. They couldn't care for Mynor in the long term but they were prepared to take him in temporarily. He was destined to return to the streets. However, this family also knew Mynor's aunt, Anna, and Anna knew her children were safe off the streets, growing up in a home and going to school. She decided to take Mynor to the home too, one of those supported by Toybox. It's as if God kept this link open to bring Mynor off the streets.

I started thinking about how God always has his hand on each one of these children and adults. Even though we don't always understand or know why bad things happen, we sometimes see tiny glimpses of how things work out. In the Bible story of Joseph, his brothers sell him as a slave. For twenty years he doesn't see them again and during that time he suffers pain, rejection and punishment for something he didn't do. He is alienated from his family, yet God is still with him. Humanly, we would look at his situation and think all was lost. But, twenty years later, God uses Joseph to save his family and to teach us all about forgiveness.

Mynor was unknown to us for the past six years and I can only imagine the pain and rejection he felt – not to mention the punishments he probably received for things he didn't do. I can also only imagine the alienation he felt from his family, but God was still there with him. God used his aunt to bring him back to a place of safety. I would not want this to happen to any child, but I think that, through it all, God sees what happens to each of the children and He still cares for each one. Until we reach heaven we will only see tiny glimpses of God working through history. Perhaps Mynor will be president of Guatemala one day and will bring forgiveness and reconciliation to its people, with the wisdom he has gained from the experiences he has had in life. It happened with Joseph. There's no reason why it couldn't happen again.

8

Bolivian Boys Build Better Lives

"A forgotten people given the chance to grown wings and fly."

Martin Smith, Delirious

Amazing stories of hope are by no means limited to Guatemala. Since my first trip to Guatemala, I have travelled to other places in the world and observed different types of projects which are helping some of the world's poorest people. From HIV/AIDS projects in Senegal, to vocational training projects in Rio de Janiero, Brazil and educational programmes in the Dominican Republic, lives are being changed and futures are being formed.

A Bolivian focus – Red Alert. Catching them early

Bolivia is considered to be the poorest country in Latin America with around two-thirds of the population defined as poor. When a child in Bolivia finds their way onto the streets of a big Bolivian city, such as Cochabamba, they are desperately looking for hope.

Research shows that the first few hours that a child spends on the street are crucial and can determine the course of what happens from that point onwards. It doesn't take long for a child on the streets to be enticed into a prostitution ring or to join a gang. Although the gang may offer them support and a sense of belonging, it is likely it will also lead to a child being introduced very quickly to drugs and crime – all part of the daily routine of survival for many street children the world over.

Giving children a way out at this point is vital but it requires teamwork. With support, local organisations can galvanise the community to really make a difference. By joining with others such as local churches, taxi drivers, station staff and bus drivers they can do all that they can to make sure that the children arriving on the streets are offered friendly help and a safe place to stay.

Building a new life off the streets

One place which is allowing some remarkable boys to build better lives for themselves is a place called Nacer. As the boys there have told me their stories, I have been struck by the common themes which come up time and time again. The stories of drug and alcohol abuse are harrowing at times, yet they explain the patterns of behaviour which the boys fall into and the very real difficulties which they experience along the way. Their stories give a real glimpse into what life is like for some of the children in Bolivia. They are also a testament to what can happen when children receive the care they need and when they are given opportunities and choices for the future.

From abuse to the streets

All the boys in Nacer are individuals and each has their own unique story, but one common theme which appears amongst the majority of their stories is that of abuse and the effects of alcoholism within their families. Antonio's account of his early life shows us the very real consequences that these children live with when life at home is not as it should be.

Antonio, aged 17 years

When I was 5 or 6 years old, my stepfather threw me out of his house because I threw a piece of slate into his belly. I did that because he was drunk and he was beating my mother in such a way that she fainted. On some occasions he almost killed her from pure beatings. The only thing I could do when he hit her was to cry or shout out so that the neighbours would hear my shouts and come to defend or save the life of my mother.

When I threw the piece of slate at my stepfather he was very drunk. After I threw it I started to run to a mountain that was near my house. I remember that there was a lake and the only thing I could hear was my stepfather running after me saying, "Never come back home again". I was on the mountain all day, so afraid of my stepfather. It was for that reason, because of fear, that I never went back to my house.

I can only begin to imagine how Antonio must have felt. As young children we look to our parents to provide the safety and security that we need. Home needs to be a place where we feel safe and where we can be protected as we grow up and prepare to move out into the world for ourselves. Antonio's environment was anything but secure. His early years of life were spent worrying about whether his stepfather would kill his mother. And, quite possibly, whether his stepfather would also attack him. Safety and security were not common feelings for Antonio; the harsh reality of life hit him very early on.

The same was true for young Marvin. Choosing street life is a huge decision for these children and they often spend a long time thinking about it before they actually make that move. But, I guess there is only so much time you can spend hiding under your bed before the decision to move out of home becomes ever more appealing.

Marvin, aged 13 years

I went to live on the streets for one reason – my father used to arrive home drunk and he would start to fight with my mum. Every time this happened, I used to hide under the bed. One day I went out with a friend and it was then that my friends said, "Let's go onto the street, we'll be OK". So I lived on the streets from that day onwards.

Difficult choices

The decision to leave home is a difficult decision in itself but the difficult choices certainly don't stop there. As the children recounted their stories it struck me that once on the streets they often ended up getting involved in things which they knew weren't helpful to them – but they did it anyway.

Pedro, aged 18 years

All that I did was to get on well with my friends, doing what they did, like for example stealing, drinking, smoking drugs and fighting. I learnt to steal, cheat, lie, fight and smoke marijuana. I felt hate for many other people. I no longer worried about my brother and my grandmother; I just took drugs and tablets to forget about them.

One of my best friends was killed. One night he died in my hands. It's something that I don't like to tell. I felt so bad that I just started to look for revenge. I knew more or less who had stabbed him. I was very scared but at the same time I did nothing to change. It was like I was hypnotised and my thoughts were incredible. When I was in my family I used to say, "I'll kill my brother and my grandmother and then I'll kill myself so we will no longer suffer in this life". I had no idea what I was thinking.

Right at this time, we had a fight with a gang for drugs. My friends killed two of the other gang members and left one almost dead. I participated in the fight. This fight was revenge for a friend. The next day the police started to investigate and all the gangs started to move away.

Marvin, aged 13 years

I lived on the streets, getting to know other friends who told me to sniff what they were sniffing. I sniffed it and I didn't go back home. I took drugs and I also went around stealing wallets and necklaces. When night came, I slept on bags and cardboard and I felt bad. Sometimes it made me want to go home. One night the police chased us from the park with sticks.

Antonio, aged 17 years

I started to save money, bit by bit, until I could buy a box to shine shoes. I started to shine shoes when I was 7 years old. The money I earned shining shoes I wasted on playing on electronic games. Sometimes I didn't eat any food because I just wanted to use the money to play on the electronic games. This was becoming my vice.

The more I understand of the childhood experiences of these children, the more I am able to see why they may choose the escape and survival methods that they do. Many of them feel worthless and lack any hope for the future. As they don't believe that they are worth anything, they place little value on their lives. At times they realise that their current choices aren't working but it is often as if they don't know how to get out of them. That is why it is so crucial for people to stand alongside them at times like this and to help them out of the situations in which they find themselves.

Building better lives

Watching the children struggle on their own on the streets is a heart-rending experience. Watching them trying to leave the streets can be equally hard at times. It is often an immensely difficult process for them, as they are torn between the life that they know and the possibility of the life that could be. Giving up addictions, leaving behind street friends and apparent freedoms isn't always easy. Support and encouragement are crucial. At points on the journey, the kids sometimes fall back into old habits or are overwhelmed by the emotions and memories of all that has happened to them, but little by little they are able to walk into the new life that can be there for the taking.

Antonio's story – Time for a change

One day I became tired of living life how it was. I decided to change my attitudes which I knew were bad. I was now 8 and a half years old. The next morning I saw a lady with an identity badge in a restaurant; she was asking for help for her home. I drew close to the lady and I asked if I could go to the home. She said "yes" and said that she herself would take me there. She took me outside the restaurant and told me to wait for a moment. I waited from the morning until nearly nightfall. She didn't come back.

One boy, who had been watching what had happened to me, told me that he knew of a home and that he could take me to that home. I spent my last night on the street and the following day I went with the boy to this home, Nacer, which is where I am now.

The first week I found it difficult to adapt to a new environment where everything was different to what I did daily on the street. No stealing, no lying, not doing bad things that I used to do on the street. Also, the home was run by Christians. When I was on the street, I didn't believe in anything, now I was learning about a God. In the second week in August, on a Sunday in 1998, I decided that I believed in Jesus and I became a Christian. I started changing my attitudes little by little and my way of thinking also began to change. Although there are many tests, temptations and failings, I have to lift myself up and carry on with my life. The desire I had when I was a boy was to be able to change my life – now I had that chance.

Family visits

When I had been in Nacer for a little while, I decided I wanted to go and visit my mother. I was excited with joy but I was also afraid of finding my stepfather drunk and beating my mother. I started praying and asking God to help me to forgive my stepfather. Thanks to God, when I arrived at my stepfather's house, everything was fine. Even though my mother didn't recognise me very well, the visit went well.

Over the next six years, I made occasional visits to my family and generally they went well. But, one day, I was in the dining room of the home and the director of the home called me and told me that there was a telephone call saying that my mother was in the hospital because she was sick and that I had to go to see her. I went to the hospital but it was too late – my mother had passed away. When I knew that my mother had passed away I didn't know what to do. It was so hard seeing my mother lying dead on a bed with many doctors and machines around her, and with lots of things in her body. At that moment, I went outside of the hospital and I started to pray that God would give me the necessary strength to get through this time of pain for the loss of my mother.

Although I had only spent five years of my life with my mother as a child and then occasional days of my youth, I had desired to share many more times with her. My mum was dead and my real father I only knew from photos. I didn't know any of my father's family or my mother's family either. All that was left for me was my two brothers. I am the youngest and my oldest brother is on the street.

Looking to the future

What I'm doing now in the home is keeping on with all my heart. I'm growing more spiritually. I like to read books which give advice on how to be a good leader. Also, I'm preparing myself for a time beyond my youth. What I want to do in the future is to help other people, as I was helped by others in my life. I would like to be a missionary. To all who are reading this, I just ask you to pray for my life and for the life of every child in a home like mine. Pray too for all those in the world who find themselves in difficulties and problems. I give thanks to God for protecting me in every moment and for what He is doing in my life. Also I give thanks to God for giving me all that I have and for giving me a good talent in music. Thanks, God!

Thank you God

The honesty with which the boys from the home Nacer talk of their present and past lives is refreshing. They know that they have made mistakes. They know that they are still not perfect. However, they also know where they are heading and the direction they want their life to take from this point onwards. If we had met these boys several years ago when they were living on the streets, addicted to drugs, committing crimes and causing trouble, I wonder what we would have thought. I wonder if we would have taken the time to see past their behaviour, the dirt of their clothes and the anger of their attitudes to see the hidden possibilities for the future.

Thank God that he sees past what is presented on the outside and He knows what we could all become. And, thank God too that there are people who are prepared to get their hands dirty in order to see children move from the darkness and imprisonment of their current situation into the freedom and joy of where life can take them. The world would be a much poorer place without them.

Pedro, aged 18 years

Since I arrived at the home I didn't want to be the same as before. I wanted to be someone who wasn't rejected by other people or beaten up by the police. The whole of the first year was difficult for me because I wasn't used to it. I always felt weak, like I couldn't do it by myself, and I kept fighting with my own strength. I didn't think anyone could help me to change and to be different.

One day I made a decision to accept Christ as my saviour. Everything changed, even the way in which I thought before was no longer the same, but I found it difficult. Now I am a new person and I want to keep going ahead. I don't want to fail my heavenly Father. Thanks to God I'm now a young person. Now that I've finished my high school education I would like to study architecture.

I would like you to pray for my life, not only for me but also for the life of every young person or child who lives on the street throwing their lives away. May God bless this home as it goes ahead. I will pray a lot that everything goes well.

9

The Story of Elisabet:
From the streets to the salon!

"Defend the cause of the weak and fatherless; maintain
the rights of the poor and oppressed. Rescue the weak
and needy; deliver them from the hand of the wicked."

Psalm 82:3–4

God's message is clear; His heart breaks for the poor, the
hurting and the lost. Not only that, the Bible clearly tells
us that God expects His people to share this concern and
to act upon it. Seeking justice and reaching out to a
broken world are often hard things to do. Such actions
can carry a high personal cost and often involve making
sacrifices. However, these sacrifices are so often worth it.

As the earlier chapters of this book have shown,
working on the streets of Latin America has been, and
continues to be, a dangerous, risky and difficult task.
Walking beside the children who choose to leave the
streets is also a hard road and things don't always work
out the way we want them to. But, change is possible. It
really is possible to right some of the wrongs we see in
our world. We haven't been able to change the whole

world but we have been able to change the lives of many street children in Latin America. Their testimonies shine out as examples of why justice is worth fighting for; their stories give us the hope to carry on.

This chapter is solely dedicated to the story of one amazing young lady, Elisabet. Among the hardships of the work, the disappointments of the children we've lost and the setbacks there have been along the way, young people like Elisabet have inspired us with their hope, challenged us with their example and encouraged us to continue to fight for justice. The children we meet on the streets are so often emotionally, physically and mentally scarred by the events of their short but difficult lives. They have so many obstacles to overcome and so many challenges to face that it is not surprising that, for some, the road to a new life seems too hard a road to walk down. However, young people such as Elisabet show that such change really is possible. When time, money and energy are poured into the lives of these kids and when people are prepared to see past the outward behaviour and instead see the inner potential, remarkable things can occur.

I have watched Elisabet grow up over the last seven years and it is my privilege to be able to share her story with you. Although a painful story in parts, it is certainly a story with a happy ending! And, more than that, it is a story which Elisabet is eager to share with you. She is so grateful to God and to His people for all that she has received and achieved over the last few years. It is her prayer that by sharing her story, people will be encouraged not only to join with others in reaching out to the poor but also to realise that there is a God who loves them and that no matter how they may be feeling, His love is available to them too.

Growing up in Puerto Barrios

Hello, my name is Elisabet and this is my story, well my story so far! I'm 20 years old at the moment and I was born in a town called Puerto Barrios which is about 500km from Guatemala City – so a long way!

Puerto Barrios is such a beautiful place – it has sandy beaches, rivers, lots of fish and a lovely climate. I loved to sit quietly outside, admiring the scenery and breathing in the fresh, clean air. I come from a big family, in fact I'm the sixth of ten brothers and sisters! That might sound like a lot of people but I really do love to be around them. My home was a very humble place, made from wood and very simple, and with none of life's luxuries such as electricity. We had very little money and would have to cook on wood, as we couldn't even afford a stove. My home had just two beds in it. I and my nine other brothers and sisters would sleep in one bed, while my mum and dad had the other. As you can imagine, it was very cramped. It was also very dark and dingy and the smell at times could be overwhelming.

I was about 8 years old when my life changed dramatically. My dad started to treat my mum really badly. He would drink really heavily and then would end up beating up my mum. All of us children were suffering and none of us were able to go to school. This was partly because my dad had no interest in sending us but also because we didn't have enough money to go. We all really wanted to study and to make our lives better. I remember sitting and crying as I watched other children walking off to school – it just didn't seem fair. We even begged our father to allow us to go to school but nothing seemed to work. Other children would call us retards or ignorant, using bad words which broke our hearts and humiliated us. They saw us just working, carrying water to houses in buckets to fill their storage butts. We could earn 5 quetzals (about 50 pence) each time we filled a water butt and each one would take about 20 buckets of water.

So that was how we grew up, with the older children supporting the younger ones. My dad was often out of work. When he could, he worked in the port at Puerto Barrios, helping off load boats when they came in. However, we did not often see any of the money that he earned.

From bad to worse

The thing I hated most about that time was the nights when my father would come home and touch me all over my body. He tried to rape me and I find it hard to remember whether or not he succeeded. I did tell my mum about it but that didn't help the situation at all. When my mum asked my dad about it, he beat her really hard with a machete which meant that she had to go to hospital. She had 18 stitches in her head – I think he wanted to kill her. When she asked my dad why he wanted to hurt his daughter, my dad said that I wasn't his daughter, that I was illegitimate.

Every day I felt sad. At times I even wanted to kill myself so that I wouldn't have to be with my family any more. I don't remember ever feeling happy at this time of my life. Sometimes I even wanted to kill my dad because I hated him so much.

One morning, after another night when my dad had abused me, I asked my mum if my dad really was my dad. I figured that if he wasn't really my dad then there wouldn't be a big problem if I killed him. My mum was crying and she told me that, if there was a God above, He knew that this man was my real father. I told my mum that I didn't think I could stay in this house any longer. One night after that, my dad abused me again. So, I prepared to leave home so that he couldn't do that to me again.

Running away

The next day, I ran away. I felt awful. I had no family to go to, only the street. I remember knocking on the door of a neighbour, asking for work in her restaurant. Amazingly, she accepted me like a daughter. I stayed with her, working in the restaurant. Most of the money I earned I took to my mum to help her and my brothers and sisters. My dad wasn't giving them anything at this time, so I felt responsible to provide. During this time, my dad attacked two of my brothers, Marvin and Walter, with a machete. The two of them left home too and were living in the streets. We did not know where, as they weren't in Puerto Barrios.

For three years, I moved from restaurant to restaurant. Unfortunately, I couldn't stay long in each place, as my dad would come to look for me – he wanted to hurt me and to cause trouble. For example, one day, he came in really drunk and broke several tables. So, I had to leave.

After about three years, when I was about 11, it didn't seem to matter any more. I had started spending many nights sleeping on the benches in the market. It was there that I met many boys and girls who were involved in various gangs. They invited me to join a gang. I decided to accept and for some time I actually felt happy - I felt like I belonged to a family at last! When one of us cried, all of us would cry because we all understood each other. There were some who had even bigger problems than mine. We hung out in discos, on the beach, in the parks, on bikes. Sometimes we would even sleep in the discos, as they stayed open until six in the morning. We smoked and we drank. At first it was just alcohol and cigarettes, but soon we started on all sorts of drugs, whatever we could get our hands on. Stuff like marijuana and cocaine. We didn't steal the drugs though – we paid for them. Some of the gang members had jobs, although I could never seem to get one – it seemed as if every door was just shut in my face.

Occasionally, I would bump into one of my older brothers. He took and sold drugs and so sometimes we would take them together. One day we decided to get tattoos – I got one on my hand and one on my arm. My younger sister Sofia also joined the group. She couldn't stay at home either because of my dad. In the end, only the three smallest were left at home; Maicol, Marilyn and Carmen. Sometimes, Sofia and I would want to visit our mum, but our dad would come running after us with a machete. I remember crying in despair. I really wanted to be close to my mum, to share my problems with her. The only way I could see her was by hiding in the grass nearby and watching her for a few minutes. Sometimes my father caught me and would burn my arms with cigarettes. Sofia also has burn scars all over her body.

A life not worth living

I started having problems with the gang. There were many fights in the streets and sometimes I had problems with the boys in the gang. When I was 13, I was kidnapped. It happened because I had hit a girl and then she had taken a photo of me. I had hit her because the gang leader had ordered me to do it. You had to do what he said or he would hit you. I didn't hit her very hard, just twice in the face, but her boyfriend wanted revenge so the two of them kidnapped me in a car.

I had reached rock bottom. I told them that it really didn't matter if they killed me – in fact, I encouraged them to kill me. I had wiped my heart clean of any thoughts of my mother, my family, God, heaven or hell. It seemed like I had no soul left.

But, the guy said to me that I was just a child and really pretty and I shouldn't be hanging around with the gang. They kept me for a night in the car, left me and then went away without doing anything to me. All I had were a few marks on my arm where they had held on to me.

I went back to the gang. When I was about 14 years old, I spent most of my time drinking and working in bars with my sister. The bars were horrible places (nothing like bars in England!). Sofia had so much hate in her heart and wanted to kill our father too. I think he had abused her and raped her a lot. It was very hard – all we had was each other.

I tried to kill myself many times during this period. I slit my wrists twice; I really, really wanted to die. The first time I tried, I passed out. My sister Sofia found me and took me to the hospital. I told her not to do that as I just wanted to die. I remember that my father came to visit me in the hospital. He was drunk, as usual. He said that if I wanted to die, he may as well help me and he started to press on the drip needle in my hand. Then my mum came to visit me. I remember her standing at the bottom of my bed, crying. I explained to her that I wanted to die. She told me that she had been crying out to God, asking him to save Sofia and me. I remembered how, when I was younger, she would hear us crying out in the night in fear, and she would ask God to save us all from the situation that we were in. But now, she was saying that she had lost faith.

There were other times when I couldn't get hold of any drugs and life seemed worse than ever; there was just no way to escape my own reality. It was then that I tried to kill myself with pills and drink. Once again, I was taken to hospital. Apparently, I was frothing at the mouth. I kept asking God, why couldn't he just let me die? Surely I had tried enough times to kill myself now. Now is the time for me to die, I told God. Kill me now, I pleaded with Him, I just need this suffering to end.

While I was in hospital, things were dreadful. I had neither drugs nor my gang friends. I was really frightened when I heard that one of my friends from the gang had been raped by another gang – supposedly 40 men had raped her at one go. She had been found in a critical state and remained in hospital for a month.

More family interaction

I left hospital and went to the home of one of my brothers, a two-hour walk from where I had been. My brother was married with two children. Although his wife was not happy about me staying in the house, my brother would always tell me that he cared for me very much and that he was always there for me. But, I still didn't feel like I had found a solution for my life.

One of my aunts came to visit me and decided to take me to a place where people would practice witchcraft. I didn't really want to go because I didn't really believe in such stuff. But my aunt insisted. She spent some time with a fortune teller and I had to sit beside her. At the end of the consultation, the woman looked at me and shouted out that she could see death in me and she told me I was going to die. She explained that she normally expected payment, but in my case she would tell me everything for free. So, I listened as she started putting her cards on the table. She told me that I had cancer of the stomach and some problems in my brain, and a whole load of other things. She told me that I wanted to kill a man but that another man would come into my life and he would be the one that would kill me. She also said that my dad wanted me dead, that I had always looked for happiness in my family but I would never find it.

I went home, but didn't pay much attention to what she had said. Well, perhaps I did. One time when I was alone in the room that I was sharing with my aunt, I felt that the room was a deep opening, like a well, and I felt that I was held by chains in a black hole. I started shouting – everything around me was black and I couldn't move for all the thick chains. When I came back to reality I was on the balcony of the second-floor room, about to throw myself to the ground below. As I was about to fall, I felt a hand grab me from behind and hold me back from falling. Whoever it was needed to be strong because I was heavy by then. I believe it was God.

As I lay there on the floor, God asked me what I was doing with my life. I told him I wanted to die but He cried and reminded me that I was just a child and not yet ready for death. I know that He saved me that day. If I had fallen, I would surely have died and not been alive today to tell you my story.

The start of something new

Time passed and I calmed down a bit and was able to give up the drugs. I decided that if there really was something more for me in this life then I didn't want to be loaded down with drugs. I wanted no more to do with the gang and all the men who had treated me so badly in the past.

I was staying with my brother when two people, Jomara and Fito, from a project called El Castillo, came to Puerto Barrios looking for my mother and father. My two brothers, Marvin and Walter, had given them details about our family. It turns out that they, Marvin and Walter, had been with El Castillo for about two years. I just happened to be visiting my dad's house that day and found Jomara and Fito there. They were trying to find my mum. My dad was really drunk and first of all I denied that I was anything to do with the family and said that my mum and dad did not live there. However, Jomara insisted that I looked like Marvin. I remember this particularly because I had not seen Marvin for about four years. For all I knew, he and Walter were dead. In fact, all the family had assumed they were dead.

They told me to call my mother so that they could talk to her as well as my father. My mother came and they confirmed that she was Marvin's mother and that they were looking after Marvin back in the city. When she heard that he was alive, she shouted out and burst into tears.

They started to tell us all about El Castillo and how Marvin and Walter were now. My mum began to plead with them for Sofia and me. She told them that we were completely lost. Somehow, they seemed to see my past life in my face. Jomara started talking to me, telling me that I needed something more in my life but that I needed help to achieve it because of all that I had gone through. I felt as if two angels were talking to me as they chatted to me about the reality of my life. They carefully explained to me that if I wanted to change they were ready and able to help me. I would be able to go with them and to be near to my two brothers. They gave me a week to decide what I wanted to do. Although it may seem like a big decision to make, I knew it was right. I said yes, and my sister Sofia decided to come with me.

Big changes in the big city!

So, a week later, Jomara and Fito returned; this time with Marvin and Walter too! They looked so good and were doing so well. I knew that going to the city would be the right thing to do. I asked Jomara to help me, to take me away from my life in Puerto Barrios. I really did want to change. My mum didn't believe me – she said that she had heard me say the same things so many times before. She just couldn't believe that I could really change. She even said that if I went, I would be back in two or three days.

However, I wasn't back in two or three days! God started changing us and changing our lives through the work of El Castillo. We came to know Jesus. This happened at a church in Zone 3 of Guatemala City which Eric and Marisol, two of the El Castillo workers, took us to each week. The pastor came to pray for me and God gave him a vision of all that had happened in my life, all the details including what my father had done to me. I figured that someone must have told him all this! He continued to pray directly with me and, in that moment, I fell to my knees and I started to cry. He reassured me that God was and is my father. In that moment, I restored my relationship with God. I received Jesus into my life and I felt the Holy Spirit touch me. I felt all my chains and burdens that I had held for so long fall away. I felt completely relaxed. After this I slept with a deepness that I had never known before in the 15 years of my life. This was November 2000.

Three weeks later, I decided to get baptised. My heart told me this was the right thing to do. I was still under attack from the devil – I was suffering from the effects of drugs and I was still struggling with my feelings for my father. I would sometimes shut myself in my room and feel like giving up. But, then I would remember what had happened. I would say to myself that I was going to keep going, keep fighting and beat the devil once and for all with the help of God.

There was no way that I was going to return to how I had been.

God helped me change in all areas of my life and I was eventually able to forgive my dad. I wrote to him telling him that I forgave him and asking his forgiveness if I had been a disobedient daughter. I explained to him that I was now a Christian and how it had changed my life. I also visited him and he saw that I had really changed. He started to cry! I had never seen him like that – my only memories of him were of being drunk. He said he was sorry for not having valued me more as a daughter and for not giving me all that I needed as a child. I had always dreamed of being a teacher and he had not done anything to allow me to realise my dream. I still pray to God for the life of my dad because he has not managed to change. He still drinks and now has no children with him and my mum has left too. He is all alone, lost in this vice because he just doesn't want to give it up.

About a year after I entered El Castillo, I started praying that Maicol and Marilyn, my little brother and sister, would be able to be with me because I feared that they might start to suffer in the same way that Marvin and I had suffered. I feared that my story might be repeated all over again. Sometimes I could not sleep; I would have nightmares about them. I shared all this with the staff of El Castillo. My prayers were answered when one day they went to collect Marilyn and Maicol. My dad was really angry when they left but this was a decision ordered by the Guatemalan judge and I know it is the best thing for them. Once they were in El Castillo, I felt much more at peace and I felt I could move forward again with my life.

Dreaming about the future

I had lots of plans and ideas of one day working with children. The family who I lived with in Shalom, the girls' home, helped me so much. Chris and Richard were just like parents to me. They gave me all the love that I didn't get from my own parents. They got me started on my education and each day when I returned from school they always greeted me with a hug and a kiss on the cheek. They would ask me how I was getting on and I felt happy to be with parents who really cared for me. I shall always appreciate everything they did for me, giving me love as if I were their own daughter. I managed to overcome all my problems and they encouraged me to learn to read so that I could begin to read my Bible. We talked loads and they helped me forgive. I was also able to ask God to help my family, including my older brothers and sisters. I just felt so blessed to be in the home with them. They helped me so much and, with them, I was able to fulfil my dreams.

One thing I wanted to do was to take part in a Bible school and they helped me to achieve this. They also helped me and encouraged me to become a teacher in the Sunday School at our church, La Fraternidad Cristiana de Guatemala, where we all worshipped each Sunday. I was so happy to be helping the children and dealing with their problems. I felt able to use what had happened in my life to help children who had problems as well as sharing God's Word with them.

It was at this church that I met my husband-to-be! All the girls from Shalom attended a house group for young people, and there I met Wilder who was a friend of the group leaders. We were friends for a year and then became boyfriend and girlfriend. Chris and Richard were the first to bless our relationship. They had confidence in me because they could see how much I had changed in my life. They knew that I was well clear of all that had happened in the past. They also knew that I wouldn't let them down and they could see that Wilder was a great young man!

Moving to independence!

When I was 18 years of age, I knew and I felt God telling me that it was time to move on in my life and to have my own family. I left Shalom, and Wilder and I got married. We now have a baby boy, named Richard Alexander (named after Richard and his son Alexander!). We live completely apart from El Castillo, living on the outskirts of Guatemala City rather than in Puerto Barrios.

I still feel sad sometimes and there are still times when I cry. I also cannot imagine how I could repay God for all that He has done for me. He has given me a husband and a baby. He has accepted me and not rejected me. I feel that I cannot repay Him with words but I intend to with my life. I want to do all I can to thank Him for the amazing miracles I have seen in the last five years of my life. He has brought me to the city and brought me to know him. I feel so happy! One of the things that I tell Him is that I will never go back. I cry, telling Him that for nothing would I return to the life I used to have.

My advice for anyone is to seek God first. I wish I had known Him when I was 8 years old, then I wouldn't have made so many mistakes in my life. It doesn't matter what age you are. It doesn't matter who you are or what your heart is like or has been.

The exact words aren't important if you don't know what to pray. Just close your eyes and tell God to take your life, and that you give it to Him. When I spoke to Him, with all my heart and in a place of humility, He accepted me and showed me an amazing future with Him. I have seen Him working in my family too. My mum has recently accepted God and started going to church. I know that He will continue changing my family.

I hope that what I have written will inspire others to seek God and reflect on His great love for all of us. Nothing is impossible for God!

The dedicated couple who Elisabet referred to in her account are Chris and Richard Rice. They have supported and loved Elisabet over the last six years and they are able to give us a glimpse into the type of love and care that is needed to bring about changes in the lives of these children. They also show us that it is often in giving that we receive so much. Chris and Richard have faced many hardships, hurts and disappointments during their work but I know that they would be the first to tell you that they wouldn't change it for the world! They have received so much back and they are so overjoyed to have had the privilege of walking alongside some amazing children. Elisabet is one of those.

Our beautiful daughter and our handsome grandson!

If Elisabet had been the only result of our work with the children of Guatemala then we would still be more than satisfied. She came to us five years ago as a sullen, uncommunicative 15-year-old teenager,

burdened with a lost childhood and memories of massive maltreatment by her parents. She could neither read nor write and knew nothing of the world or how life should be.

We had actually met with her and her sister Sofia a couple of times before they came to Shalom, the home that we ran for teenage girls who had left a life on the streets or horrific home circumstances. We were quite apprehensive about taking charge of a girl who seemed pretty convinced that all adults were the enemy, with men being particularly evil.

God moved in a mysterious way, as ever! We were looking for a way to break through the tough outer skin and find the child inside. It happened - after less than two weeks - but in a "bad news, good news" sort of way. We had decided to take all the girls in our care to see some spectacular fireworks in the city - put on each Christmas by a local business. The fireworks were fantastic and it was great to see their faces as they took it all in. However, there was a crowd crush at the end and we got separated. Everyone but Elisabet was reunited by 11pm and we spent a hectic night searching. Praise the Lord, she had managed to find a friendly (and there's a miracle!) policeman and spent a safe night in a police station. She even managed to explain to the police where Shalom was (another miracle considering the short time that she had been with us and the fact that previously she had barely been outside her home town of Puerto Barrios).

You can only start to imagine the hugs, kisses and tears when she returned to our home the next day. Back together once again, we shared words of love and happiness. For us, it was just as if one of our own children had been lost and at that moment it began to sink into Elisabet's heart and mind that we weren't there to be her guardians, we were there to be like parents to her - and not just parents, but parents very different from the ones she had left behind in Puerto Barrios. On top of that she inherited a brother and sister in Alex and Bryony (our own two children) and learnt that brothers can be friends and not someone that kicks you about, abuses you and lives by crime.

From that moment it seemed that there was no stopping her. We still dealt with childish tantrums, but, hey, she'd missed out on that bit as well! Imagine childish tantrums with a hormonal attitude – oh boy! She struggled with her education, but we were the proudest "parents" ever when she finished her first year and could at last read and write, albeit a little ponderously. Two years later she finished her primary education. The rest is history.

We look at her now and it is so difficult to recall those first days. She is a beautiful young lady, literate, skilled in her chosen profession of hairdresser-come-beautician. She has a husband who adores and cares for her and the most gorgeous baby boy in the world (OK, so we may be a bit biased!). And she has completely broken the cycle of abuse and neglect; the way she cares for her baby is a model for any mother, worldwide.

We don't claim the glory for the 180 degree revolution in Elisabet's life – God gets that. But, we are so happy to have been a part of it and, at the end of the day, we now have a handsome little grandson called Richard Alexander. That suits us just fine!

10

The Kids Give to Others

"Few will have the greatness to bend history itself; but each of us can work to change a small portion of events, and in the total of all those acts will be written the history of this generation."

Robert F. Kennedy

Watching a street child receive the support they need to be able to return to their family, move into a foster home or take up a place in a small, family-style home is brilliant and is something that will always stay with those who have worked as part of the teams in Latin America. However, the story doesn't stop there. Helping a child to leave the streets is merely the beginning of the process. Although the rest of the process can have its challenges, disappointments and frustrations, it can also be hugely rewarding. It has been a real privilege for me to watch so many children 'grow up' over the past seven years. Some of them have grown up and 'flown the nest', so to speak, others are now seven years older and hitting those teenage years. In many ways they are just like ordinary kids in England would be but in other ways they are so very different. Their experiences shape who they are and who they want to become. Many of those who meet them are struck by their desire to learn, to give and to make a difference to their countries, to other young people and to a world of need. Their stories, lives and testimonies have had an impact on the lives of many that they have come into contact with. Not only have the staff and volunteers that have worked with them been inspired and encouraged, but so have many others around the world who have read and heard their stories. It is clear that God is using these restored children and young people to bring more hope into those places of the world where there can seem to be no hope.

The Emmanuel boys – Hazel Ireland, former Toybox gap year student

Shortly after Andres and Giovani arrived in the home Emmanuel, they and the other boys in the home organised a cabaret-style show for the house parents and some visitors from England. The boys spent countless hours rehearsing in secret, whispering plans to one another, until the day finally arrived. Guests were seated around a 'stage' in the living room, and a captivated audience watched open-mouthed as the boys performed their sketches, songs and dramas. Within minutes, the boys had the viewers in fits of laughter and tears, as their clown impersonations, slapstick comedy routines and dramatic songs transcended the language barriers in the room. The culmination of the events was a song, sung by all the boys in the home. They had chosen a song, recently released by a popular Christian band,

and changed the lyrics to express their heartfelt thanks to God and to their new house parents for the chance to lead a new life. The words of the song went like this:

I arrived at Emmanuel
With a desire to learn
And to be able to change my life
The dreams that I once had,
Goals I wanted to reach,
They have finally begun to come true.
And if there is one thing that I have learnt
It's that Jesus is my final goal
And this is more than just a passing phase.
I will love you, Lord
I will love you with all my heart
Until I can say, like your servant Paul,
I have finished the race,
the victory I have won.

What a moment, as the song finished, and the teary silence dissolved into overwhelming applause. We witnessed the transformation of a group of boys whose lives had literally been saved from the pit to a wonderful new life of hope.

Teenagers who offer to wash up!

Many people who work with the kids are struck by their levels of care for each other, and for those outside of their new 'family'. Lorenzo is a real example of this. Lorenzo used to work on the city rubbish dump in Guatemala from early morning to late at night, collecting large rocks, which he had to pile in one corner of the dump. His father had died when he was about one and his alcoholic stepfather and mother were constantly abusing him verbally and physically. One night he came home and his mother started yelling at him. Finally, in her rage, she took her hot iron and branded Lorenzo on his arm, burning him badly. For Lorenzo this was the last straw and he left the shack which was his home and began living on the streets. That was eight years ago and Lorenzo is now firmly established in one of the homes which Toybox is supporting. A practical joker, Lorenzo has a deep throaty laugh which is as infectious as his smile. He was born to be a clown and if there is ever water around you can guarantee that it will be Lorenzo who will begin throwing it!

Someone I know recently told me of her experiences with Lorenzo. As a female volunteer in a boys' home, she found herself doing a lot of clearing up, especially after mealtimes. As she was attempting to wash up one evening, Lorenzo stopped her and said, "I know you are very good and helpful, but I will do the washing up tomorrow, I don't want you doing it". She was shocked at what a thoughtful and caring thing had been said from someone who had lived the life he had, and wondered how many boys his age would have said that if she had been working in Britain.

Kids help clear up after Hurricane Stan

On 5 October 2005, Guatemala was severely affected when Hurricane Stan hit Latin America. Nearly two weeks of torrential rainfall caused massive landslides across the country. Hundreds of people were killed and whole villages were covered by massive mudslides. In addition to this, thousands of houses were washed away and many others were left too damaged or dangerous to be lived in. Many roads were destroyed and crops and food production were both severely affected.

In the wake of this natural disaster, many communities were desperately in need of help, support and recovery. Young people from a project supported by Toybox took part in some of the recovery work. Their compassion for others in need was a challenge to those around them. They know what it is like to have very little and they are acutely aware of the very real impact that an offer of help can make in a time of desperation. Here's what they had to say about their involvement in the project.

Norma, aged 13 years

It was great to go and help build toilets in Patzun. I felt very happy to be able to help other people who were in need. What had most impact on me during the time in the towns was that they didn't even have toilets. Something I learned was that we must help others who need help.

Bryan, aged 15 years

When we arrived, the first thing that I thought was how needy the people were. Then I felt happy to have arrived there because I knew I would be able to give a little of what God has given me. I know that helping other people makes me realise that I was also helped by others. I believe that what I did, I did to demonstrate that I love them, even though I don't know them. I know that God will bless me some day – I won't receive what I gave, but something more special.

The theme of our camp this year was "What I have, I give you". I was happy because I shared with others and we were able to help build toilets to improve the hygiene for the people there.

I also give thanks to those who help us because they have taught us to serve those in need. We could see the smiles of the people when we had finished their toilets. I felt good. After we had finished, we were taken to a water park which is four hours from the capital. We had lots of fun. I had a great day and was able to share it with the homes, like a family.

Matteus, aged 12 years

It was good and an honour to have helped people. The people in that place were very poor and they needed a lot of help. I saw the faces of the people when we arrived to help and they were very happy. I also realised that I must value what I have.

Cristian, aged 17 years

One thing which had an impact on me was when the young people from my home were eating fruit and sweets. The other children watched with a desire to taste and enjoy the fruit. I and some of the others shared our fruit with the young children. I felt happy for what I did, and through this experience, I have started valuing the support I get from my home even more. Also, I will take more care using water, as I saw that the people there had to walk 1km to obtain water to drink or use to cook with.

Article from Wilfred, aged 17 years

In writing this article, it made me think of a lot of what I saw and I still remember clearly the communities we worked with when we went to Patzun. I have this place in my mind and in my prayers – seeing the needs of the people there, it made me think of the blessings I have to be where I am today.

There were some steep hills where I never thought people would be living. There we found Mr Marcelino, a man of about 45 years of age, but with a smile on his lips telling us thank you. He was helping with the building of the little houses for the toilets. I left this place with a satisfaction in my heart. Even though my body was so tired, my heart was full of a good vibe because I could do something for someone else that I never thought I would even see. It also filled me with satisfaction to see others from the homes working hard, but always with smiles on their faces, giving thanks to God for the privilege of serving. I hope this won't be the first and last time we do this, because we want to feel more useful every day, to serve our neighbours.

It is often a humbling experience to see the kids serving others; knowing where they have come from and realising what potential they have for the future. Of course, when it comes to the future, the most important thing is that they are free to make the choices that they think are the best for them. Just like parents in the UK, those of us who know and work with the kids may have our own hopes and aspirations for how their lives will turn out. But, in the end, the most that we can do is simply provide the support and care that they need and then to allow them to take the opportunities which lie ahead of them, if and when they want to. At the end of the day, whatever they do, our prayer for them is that they will be happy, healthy and content – that will do just fine!

Helping kids who are just like I used to be

As the years go by we are increasingly able to see the fruits of our labours in terms of young people moving on into independent lives. There are times when this process completely exceeds our expectations and the ability of the young people to turn around their lives and to fight for justice for others is simply breathtaking.

Located in Bolivia is a man who has had a real impact on those he meets. Now in his late forties, Erick is a softly spoken, measured and gentle man. Upon meeting him you would never realise just where he had come from. He is living proof that nothing is impossible for God. Here is his story in his own words.

Not your ideal start in life

I was 8 years of age when I started to see the reality in which my parents were living. We lived in poverty. My parents were witches and they were more dedicated to their clients than they were to us. I had two siblings and we all shared the same room as my parents. We saw many bad things through this time. We got to know how to carry out rituals which surprised and frightened us at the same time. We heard horrifying noises as they involved us in their acts of witchcraft with rabbits and with black roosters.

My mum became ill. There was no doctor available to give her the necessary assistance. She died young. My dad was an alcoholic and he started me off drinking alcohol. When I was 10 years of age, I left home and began to live on the streets. I drank more and more alcohol and I would sometimes steal to get the money I needed.

From bad to worse

One time, on the street, when I was 11 years of age, I ended up in a hostel where they treated me very badly. It was a place of torment, punishment and crying; I was only a child and I really couldn't stand it. I needed help and protection but no one gave me even one word of encouragement. I was dying inside my heart. Inside of myself I said that if one day I would be able to work in a home like this I would want it to be really good. I would fight to try to help all the children who are going through the same difficulties so that there wouldn't be violence.

Prison conditions

I left the hostel when I was 17 and I went out onto the streets again. One day I was arrested by the police. This was another painful and sad experience for me. While I was in custody I was tortured. They used to tie me up with a rope or turn me upside down. I was hit with a stick and with cables and other worse things than that. They even beat me with their guns.

By the age of 23 I was back on the streets again. I

became accustomed to living an irresponsible life which was out of control and disordered.

Meeting my wife

When I was about 34 years of age I met Ingrid, the lady who was to become my wife. She had similar problems to me. She took drugs and drank alcohol and she also left home when she was young and lived on the streets. She very quickly became my girlfriend, she became pregnant and we married.

I mistreated my wife and inflicted many injuries upon her. I usually used blunt objects like sticks and stones, but sometimes I would use sharp objects like knives which would destroy parts of her body. Ingrid suffered so much abuse and had so much pain and bitterness within her that she decided to contract one of her friends to stab me with a knife. It almost cost me my life.

A time of change

Even after the stabbing and all that happened, Ingrid didn't abandon me. She searched for me in the hospital and she took me back to our house where she took care of me. That same afternoon, she heard voices on the street and she went out to ask the people for help. The people she met were missionaries and they said that they would come back very early the next day to visit us. They found me lying down on a bed made of mud and stones. They cried out to God for my wounds. As they prayed for me, I saw an opening dividing the sky and in the middle of it was Jesus. He was so big all over and bright. He stretched his arms like he was saying 'Come'. It was at that time that my life changed.

Learning to serve

I left that place which was filled with evil and I started to help the missionaries with their work. I helped them to give out rice milk and to read the Bible. I learnt how to pray every day. Ingrid and I also learnt how to work with the children and adolescents. We worked as educators in a centre for two years which really helped us with that.

Now things are very different. My wife and I run a small home called "Little David", where children from the streets are able to build a new life. I am now able to do what I could only dream of when I was 11 years of age and living in that hostel. Thanks be to God for all he has done.

Although the changes in Erick were dramatic, they certainly weren't easy. As he comments, "It isn't easy to leave street life; it is a battle". However, it is a battle which he is certainly winning. Those who visit "Little David" are struck by what a normal and relaxed place it is. It is certainly a home rather than an institution. The boys freely wander around, playing football, enjoying being together and acting as a real family.

Simply spending time in Erick's house and with his family was profoundly humbling. On a practical level, Erick and Ingrid have created a wonderful home for the children they are caring for. On a spiritual level, his sense of God's work in his life is evident in everything about him.

Andy Stockbridge, Toybox Chief Executive

Life certainly has its ups and downs and we certainly don't want to diminish the real difficulties and challenges that exist for the children and young people who live on the streets and who have suffered so much. However, at the same time, we do also want to celebrate the very real changes and successes that we can see in the lives of so many who have managed to take hold of the opportunities on offer and who are fighting for something better, not only for themselves but for others too. And, we certainly want to give the glory to God for all He has done in their lives. These experiences and testimonies tell us that miracles were not just for Bible times – the God of today is still the God of the impossible.

11

And the Story Goes On

"The stories in this book are not meant to cause pity.
Jesus never treated people with pity; He always
responded with love, grace, power and commitment.
The stories in this book are not meant to make you feel
good, but to call you to action."

Nicky Cruz

As I have written this book, I have cried for the children
and wept over the injustice. I have shouted at God and
asked Him why. I have not found easy answers or simple
comfort but I have found a peace in Him. It has not been
easy to write but I would have found it more difficult to
have left these stories untold. As I have written, I have
been challenged to reflect on all that I have learnt and
experienced through my years of work with street
children. I realise that when I first went to Guatemala it
was with a desire to give; it was my sacrifice, or so I
thought. The reality was that, although through God's
grace I was able to give, I actually received so much more
than I ever gave. I also learnt many lessons along the way,
lessons that I need to take on board, lessons which need
to affect the way that I live.

Cultivating a spirit of thankfulness

I recently met up with a friend who had been to South America to visit a project working with some of the poorest communities who were living in makeshift urban dwellings on the edge of a city. She recounted the story of one of her encounters with a young woman named Claudia.

Life for Claudia had been one difficulty after another. Growing up in poverty and with no education, Claudia had needed to learn how to be very independent in order just to survive. Home was a makeshift shack located in a growing community that had found some land which they could use for a while, well, at least until the authorities decided that they couldn't stay there any longer. Claudia was used to such uncertainty – that's just how life could be. Her shack had no running water, with the exception of the rain that would leak through the roof whenever there was a downpour. Claudia had recently been raped and was expecting a baby. She was naturally worried about the future and about what that would hold for her. How would she manage to feed both herself and her baby? It was at this time that Claudia came into contact with a charity housing project which offered her some assistance. Claudia qualified for help and waited for her turn to come. A few months later, just after her baby had been born, Claudia was able to move into a small dwelling in another community. By our Western standards, her new home was nothing special. In fact it was a very simple one-room affair, but it was a distinct improvement on the home she had come from. This dwelling was made of breeze blocks and it had a roof which didn't leak. It was also located on land which the charitable organisation had paid for, so there was no fear of eviction. My friend visited Claudia shortly after she had moved in. From my friend's perspective, Claudia's new home left a lot to be desired. She turned to Claudia and asked her how she felt about her new home. Immediately, and with complete sincerity in her voice, Claudia said the words, "I can truly say that I am content".

The words 'I am content' are not something that we often hear in our own society, which is full of the materialistic quest for more and better things. Our lives are bombarded with marketing and advertising encouraging us to buy the latest of everything. Yet, do we really need all those things and will they really make us happy?

I am continually challenged by the spirit of contentment and thankfulness that people like Claudia show. Among the people I have met who have had so little I have seen more thankfulness and gratefulness than I have seen anywhere else. Perhaps because these people know what it is to have nothing, they also know and appreciate the full value of every small thing that they ever have. Perhaps too because they understand only too well the fragility of life, they are also able to truly cherish people while they are here with them. Their example causes me to question how much I take for granted. Many of the people I met in the shanty town areas I worked in were unsure whether they would have enough food for their families on a day-to-day basis. Each day that they had food was a day to be grateful, a day to give thanks. For me there is not that uncertainty. I take it for granted that I will be able to provide more than enough food for myself. It's not just about food either; it stretches much beyond that to things such as clothes, belongings, holidays and leisure activities. These are things which I expect to have as part of my life. In many ways I have learnt to take them for granted. However, I have a choice to look at it differently. I can choose to truly value those things, to try not to take them for granted and to cultivate an attitude of thankfulness. Valuing the small things and being grateful for all we have isn't about ignoring and denying the hard things of life – of course they still exist. However, a grateful heart can help us to cope with the harder things. It can encourage us to keep perspective not only within our lives, but also as part of our global community.

Never give up hope of a brighter tomorrow

With youthful enthusiasm, I used to believe that we could change the world. I guess I still want to believe that is true but as the years have gone by I have become increasingly aware that making the dreams of youth come true is massively more complicated than I could ever have imagined. There is no denying that our world is a complex and dysfunctional place. Most evening news broadcasts are filled with details of wars, disasters, crimes, injustices, famines – the list could go on. It can feel like things are just too much of a mess for there really to be a brighter tomorrow.

You have probably noticed a recent increase in environmentally-based adverts that tell us that we need to take a personal responsibility for the way that we live. We are encouraged to recycle more, to turn down our heating, to save water, to insulate our houses and to walk or cycle to work. The clear message that these adverts give is that what we do matters. Our actions have an impact – we can make a difference.

My experiences with Toybox have shown me that while we may not be able to change the whole of the world, we can and have been able to play a part in changing the whole world of some very special children and young people in Latin America. Those changes have only been possible because of the involvement and commitment of many people. Some people have faithfully prayed for the children or have given financially to support the work, others have worked or volunteered with Toybox in the UK and of course there are those from Latin America who have dedicated their lives to working with and caring for the children on a daily basis. Whatever they have given or whatever they have done, each person's contribution has been vital. All parts of the team are necessary for things to work and for change to happen. There is still a long way to go but change has been possible and for that reason I can continue to believe that there is hope for a better tomorrow for other children and young people too.

I would encourage you, as you look at a broken and hurting world, not to allow the scale of the problems to overwhelm you. Instead, look to the things that you can do, wherever and whenever that may be. Whether we like it or not, our actions and choices really do have an impact on those around us and on our world as a whole. We need to choose what type of an impact that will be and what type of legacy we will leave behind. Choosing to make our impact a positive one is likely to require some sacrifices on our part and no doubt we will all continue to make some mistakes along the way. But each and every day we have the chance to learn from those mistakes, to move forward and to celebrate and enjoy the blessings which can come from serving others and seeing God at work in our world of need.

Appreciate the potential in others

Prior to meeting and getting to know some of the people in Latin America, I saw charity very much as 'us' and 'them'. We gave money, we had the answers, we knew how life should be; all they needed to do was to receive. It didn't take long for my opinions on this to change. Although we can be a part of the process of development and change in Latin America, it certainly isn't only about us. The key to Latin America's future lies very much with the people of Latin America.

Towards the end of 2005, I met a young man from Venezuela by the name of Harry. Along with nine other young people from around the world, Harry was taking part in the two-year study which the United Nations was doing into violence against children. I was very impressed by this young man. Although only 19 years of age, Harry had a firm grasp on what he felt the young people of Latin America needed and he had the ability to communicate that not only to other young people but also to adults in positions of power. As this book began to develop, I asked Harry if he would like to write something for me about what he thinks about his continent and how he thinks change could happen. Here are some snippets of what he had to say.

The future of my continent

Latin America is full of large and complex issues of inequality. However, because of this it is also full of initiatives which pursue equal opportunities, social justice and peace as ways of life, rather than as privileges or prizes given by chance. Perhaps all these initiatives fail to reduce the large problems of inequality, injustice and violence in the way that our towns expect and in the time that they long for, but the existence of these initiatives are deeply positive signs. They indicate that our towns are awakening, that our towns are eager for justice, equality and peace and that they will not rest until they obtain them. These signs, these efforts in the middle of so much inequality and violence, mark out a different way, which strengthens us and which lights the way ahead.

Without doubt, the youth of Latin America and the world play a key role in this process of transformation and in the search for the construction of just, egalitarian and peaceful living conditions. I am convinced that youthfulness is about more than a date of birth or an age. Youth is when the generous impulse of our heart carries us towards the achievement of our goals, ideals and dreams. Youth is when we live the smile, the tear, the pain and the happiness of others as our own. Youthfulness is found in spirit, thought and action.

As youths, we have the difficult task of learning and growing through our mistakes while also building on our strengths. We also need to value the successes of previous generations, since this is what will give us the sensation of moving forward rather

than starting from scratch. We also need to remember what Latin America is. Latin America is, without doubt, more than a place for commercial and adventurous tourism. It is also a lot more than merely a place for donations from other continents. Latin America is a bank of spiritual, natural and human wealth that refuses to die, like the legendary bird Phoenix, which is reborn from its ashes.

As Harry says, Latin America has so much more than we may see when we simply look at the surface. Yes, it has its problems, its difficulties and its issues; no one would want to deny that. But, that really is only part of the story. There is so much potential within that continent. Some of it is well hidden among the poverty of the streets and the massive city rubbish dumps but that doesn't mean that it is any less real. What Harry and many others like him need is the support and opportunity to develop their natural, spiritual and human resources. For the time being at least, this is where we come in.

Being part of their story

Perhaps as you've journeyed through this book you've wondered how you can be part of the story. Perhaps you've questioned how you can play your part. Organisations such as Toybox provide many ways for people to respond at whatever level is appropriate for them. Many people like to respond with financial support and through child sponsorship schemes this can be combined with a personal link to an individual child. In this way you can not only give children a real chance at life, but you can learn more about them and encourage them along the way. They love to know that there are people on the other side of the world who are interested in them and who care about their future. Relationships are so important to all of us and both sides benefit through schemes such as these.

Another very valuable but often hidden response is to pray for the children and for those who are working with them. We can't all travel to Latin America but we can all pray to the God of the universe who holds the whole of the world in His hands. He knows each one of the children by name and He knows the real difficulties and challenges of the situations in which they find themselves. Keeping in touch with organisations like Toybox can inform your prayers as you receive regular updates and information on what's happening.

The other key way that people can choose to be part of the story is to really get in on the action for themselves. Volunteers are crucial. They help us to spread the word, they represent the children at events and they motivate others to get involved.

Whatever we choose to do it is good to think about how we can fill the gap and be part of the amazing stories of hope in the lives of these children. As we look to the future we are convinced that more and more children will also be helped and we look forward to being able to share these stories with you.

God's love in action

These amazing stories of hope are very much an account of God's love in action. It is God's love that motivates us to help these children and we want to give God the glory for each and every 'success' story that you have read. In the first three verses of Psalm 40 it says these words:

I waited patiently for the Lord;
he turned to me and heard my cry.
He lifted me out of the slimy pit,
out of the mud and mire;
He set my feet on a rock
and gave me a firm place to stand.
He put a new song in my mouth,
a hymn of praise to our God.
Many will see and fear
and put their trust in the Lord.

For many of the children and young people we have helped, this could describe their story. They have been taken from the mud and the mire of life, their feet have been set on a rock and they have been given a firm place to stand. Jesus has made a difference. It is my prayer that many who read and hear of this may also see it for themselves and may put their trust in God. Our God is living and active in our world and these stories of hope cause us to worship Him more.

And the story goes on

The children and young people who have contributed to this book represent so many more just like them throughout Latin America: children and young people with so much potential and with so much to give; children and young people whose rights are being compromised and whose future may look bleak but for whom change can be possible. It is for and about these young people that these stories were written.

The stories of pain and abuse challenge us to consider the ways in which we live and gently nudge us to think about how we need to respond. The amazing stories of hope shine out and encourage us that all is not lost in our world – there really are glimmers of light in the darkness. These stories also encourage us to be thankful for all we have and to see that it is often in giving that we receive the most. Journeying alongside these children is a real adventure. It is never simple or straightforward but it is certainly worth it. The smiles and freedom of the children cannot be measured in the number of prayers we have prayed or the number of pounds we have spent. We would never want to put a price on that.

I hope that you have enjoyed getting to know some of the amazing children and young people of Latin America through their words in this book. I really look forward to seeing what happens to them all over the next five, ten, even 20 years. Maybe one day they will be writing their own books!

Contact details

We hope you have enjoyed reading this book.

If you would like to find out more about Toybox, you can visit the Toybox website at www.toybox.org

If you would like to write to Angela you can contact her at:

Toybox
PO Box 660,
Amersham,
Bucks.
HP6 5YT.

Or by email to info@toybox.org

Thank you in advance for your interest in the street children of Latin America. Together we really are able to make a difference in their lives.